ANCHOR BOOKS

INSPIRATIONS FROM

CENTRAL ENGLAND

Edited by

David Foskett

First published in Great Britain in 1996 by
ANCHOR BOOKS
1-2 Wainman Road, Woodston,
Peterborough, PE2 7BU

SB ISBN 1 85930 305 6
HB ISBN 1 85930 300 5

Foreword

Anchor Books is a small press, established in 1992, with the aim of promoting readable poetry to as wide an audience as possible.

The poems in *Inspirations From Central England* represent a cross-section of style and content.

These poems are written by young and old alike, united in their passion for writing poetry.

I trust this selection will delight and please the authors from *Central England* and all those who enjoy reading poetry.

David Foskett
Editor

CONTENTS

THE HIDDEN POOL

Quite by accident
I discovered the pool
whilst walking in the woods.

Although I knew the area well
I hadn't been aware
the pool existed!

Suddenly, there it was before me
the water mostly shaded
by surrounding trees, and,
lit only on the far bank
by penetrating rays
of the setting sun.

The water was perfectly calm,
giving no hint of its depth,
or of any life
beneath the unruffled surface.
The thought crossed my mind -
'still as a millpond.'

There was absolutely no sound,
even the air held its breath.
Spreading branches of the trees
were motionless, against
the backcloth of the sky -
no sight or sound of bird or insect.

Difficult to know how long I stood there
it seemed that life itself was suspended.
The intense quiet became unbearable.
I turned and ran, anxious to prove
I was not a captive part of the scene,
relieved that I had the ability to do so.

Pamela Terry

NUNS WOOD

In the wood upon the hill
A figure stands alone and still.
She awaits the day to come
When her time on Earth is done.

Her shadowed figure watches while
A passing walker climbs a style.
Pipe in mouth, stick in hand,
He stops to view surrounding land.

He does not see her by the tree
And passes on, his thoughts on tea.
No-one sees her any more.
She disobeys Earth's mortal law.

The noise of rooks fills the sky,
They swoop and dive with mournful cry.
Night is falling all around.
Now she drifts without a sound.

When day breaks and rooks soar high,
She wishes for her soul to fly.
But still she stands beside the tree,
Embalmed in silent misery.

S Till

THE HOWLING PURSUER

In the forest of darkness,
Being pursued by a hungry wolf,
That takes flight when near to it's prey
And pounces on to my back,
Then he slips down clawing it.

The blood begins to pour
And like a Vampire the Wolf sucks it up
Draining all the life from my body.

The Wolf then howls his song of victory,
Then turns his back and runs off into the distance,
On the prowl of something else he can stalk.

At this point my imagination changes course again
Into another fantasy world,
And the Wolf can sleep once again.

Gemma Holdsworth (16)

TEARS OF SAINT LAWRENCE

Up into a darkened sky attracted by the light
My eyes can see some falling stars
As they travel through the night
A momentary vision then they disappear from sight
And I wonder if they'll fall to earth tonight

The sky was full of meaning for the people long ago
A display sent from the heavens which set the sky aglow
And from the constellation a figure did appear
And they said it was Saint Lawrence
Who returns this time each year.

Saint Lawrence was a Christian and they tell of how he died
They chained him to a burning grid
And they say that martyr cried
But he never cried for mercy even though he died in pain
He cried cos he was happy he would meet the Lord again.

Michael Haestier

MOTHER

Mamma, Mamme, Mummy, Mum, Mums
an old distant echo playing in my mind
Latin lessons of younger College's days
Sweet child's words disguised from our ancestors.

'Mater' the real word, the parent Mother
the Mother of our loved ones, of our future.
Inscribed in our hearts and souls in all
our breaths, in the mirror of our eyes.

No thoughts of parenthood in those far away days
Just games and laughter of lost sweethearts
When Mother then was simply our Mother
The woman in the house running after our socks.

Nearly four years my age as my mother reached another world
No understanding of love and cry because of a cut finger
With each new year a different look of sadness
Now the grey hairs understand the loss.

Today life has gifted me with a new life
a little bundle of joy and a new mother
What happiness to see my little son reaching
for his Mother's smile to stop his awaken cry.

Jealous I am of their special unity
embraced into each other, love and security
I, rest aback and watch over like a father
awaiting my turn for a game of roughness.

I will fight and toil and keep their lives together
thank you my darling, I say, but words are never enough
to feel their smile full of happy laughter
that's all I need for my life to succeed.

You are the mother I love and will cherish
until my eternal days.

Ludovico Scaletta

4

IN BEDS

Bedfordshire is neither there, nor here
Still struggling for size and living in fear
Of assimilation by neighbours, bigger and mean,
And sits quietly bewildered, betwixt and between.

Beds is like Belgium but on a county scale:
Thundered through endlessly by road and by rail,
Merely glanced at by travellers amid absent thoughts
En route to better-known and more distant resorts.

Beds lies uneasily, against the grain
Being neither Midlands nor South, she feels the strain
Her rivers run north, her commuters stream south
Daily out-county, towards London's vast mouth.

So what's to be seen in unnoticed Beds?
She makes her own cars, brews beer with good heads;
Has Woburn and Whipsnade, makes hats from straw plait -
Though flamboyance is certainly not a strong trait.

Bedford has Bunyan, Elstow its Moot,
There are clappers and downs and a pre-Roman route,
And cereal bars by the ton are still made
Near the old market town of - yes - Biggleswade.

You can fly, you can glide, or balloon or float
- In a gondola of course, not a ship or a boat -
For, if she's missing the sea, Beds does have the air
And only at Cardington are there hangars to spare.

Away from Wrest Park, the Abbey and Hoo
Are many more places really lovely to view
In this county, undemanding and sometimes mistook
Where it's always worth having a closer look.

P J Savage

OF FETES AND FETISHES

Eeh, wot a wunderful day I've 'ad,
Me feet are in ribbons, me bunion's bad,
But I've eaten me fill of popcorn and fudge,
Candy floss, lollipops - now I can't budge.
I've tommed the tombola and won lots of gin . . .
Funny 'ow just a drop makes me 'ead spin.

The pet show was quite an event to be seen,
Dogs, bunnies and mice all over the green.
A big notice says 'Keep your dog on a lead'
But you'd never believe the place one dog had peed -
There stood the Vicar, all proper and prim,
But a damp trouser leg soon shifted 'is grin!
Must 'ave been the excitement that all proved too much,
But somebody opened the door of an 'utch.
In went a Jack Russell and out popped a rabbit,
(Well you know they're renowned for this terrible 'abit?)
A scream from the crowd and a flurry of fur,
The whole dreadful incident passed in a blur.
One rosette, 'alf an ear and a whisker or two . . .
Amazing the damage Jack Russells can do.

Time for a bun and a nice cup of tea
But 'ow it always tastes more like gnat's wee?
I know what it is - I've seen 'ow they do it,
(Our old Mothers' Union knew 'ow to stew it.)
Now they just drop it in and whip it out quick,
Then 'ang it to dry - it's quite an old trick.

Prizes galore they 'ad in the raffle,
Me whole pension spent and not one did I snaffle.
Time to go 'ome, me bunions are bad,
But, eeh, wot a wunderful day I've 'ad.

Bridget Fraser

EVERDON BROOK

Thoughts flow to Everdon Brook
And gentle backwaters of days long ago
In the still pools let's take a look
For the minnow that didn't show

The commando tree up Everdon Stubbs
Was to us all a sheer delight
Crawling on hands and knees through scrub
Before climbing to dizzy heights

A battle for dug out and watchtower
Was fought near mantles heath
These bastions tested many an enemies willpower
But remain forever out of their reach

The arches like a sort of drawbridge
Provided us with endless fun
Up over the side to stand on the ridge
Before dropping below and then run

As winter approached sledges were ready
Grass hill was a venue for some
For those less steady like yesterday's Eddie
There was always the cresta run

As I look back on those days far away
The colours are blue not grey
Positive thoughts create a clear sky outlook
On the long winding road from Everdon Brook

Barry Cox

REMINISCENCE

I left my heart on a heathered hill,
By a burn bubbling down to the restless sea.
I left my heart and it beats there still,
Grieving and pining and calling to me.

I left my heart in the mountain skies,
On the golden wings of an eagles flight.
I left it absorbing those wild plaintive cries,
Piercing my soul in the still of the night.

I left it suspended above the ravine,
Where a gallant mare soared with her chieftain to fame.
I left it where cavalry soldiers were seen,
Applauding brave Wallace revering his name.

I left a heart broken where my father rests,
And I heard his soft brogue gently quelling my fears.
I left it restored where the nightingale nests,
For I know he awaits as our joyful day nears.

I left my heart there with a burning desire,
To stroll once again where the piper's lament.
When that magical sound turns the blood into fire,
For the last serenade as my life span is spent.

Frank Smiley

CAGED

I sit in a cage alone,
A mirror and a ladder,
My only escape from boredom
Food and drink are plentiful,
But I yearn for freedom

My reflection is my only friend,
Gazing out of the window
I see other feathered creatures,
But they would harm me,
I am an alien here.

My land is far away
I will never fly free.
My wings will not feel
The warmth of the sun,
Or the tropical breeze.

The branches of exotic trees,
Are but a distant memory,
No nest building for me,
For I have no mate,
I sit in a cage alone.

Jenny Whitehead

A TORMENTED SOUL

I live I die, I laugh I cry,
I do not know the reason why,
For in the past I've found a way,
To cover up and pave the way,
To a new corner of my mind,
Where I am power overall.
Pain comes it goes, I ask it why,
But never does it reply,
Of life of which I have no part,
For I can never give my heart.

My blood is red but has no past,
For life tomorrow I was cast.

Wendy Carn

OUR WORLD

Our world is full of beauty,
Where're you cast your eye;
On land or sea or mountains,
Or in the lofty skies.

All forms of life are found there,
And each one plays a part,
Like actors, they're performing,
To make a work of art.

God bids us all as humans,
To care for everything;
Not least, the tiny falling bird
That will appear in Spring.

We stand in awe and wonder,
As all strive to survive,
The fish, the ant, and elephant,
And bees around their hive.

If we have done our duty,
As God would have us do;
We'll leave this world of beauty,
For those who follow, too.

Angela Constable

I OFTEN TALK

I often talk
Of how I walk
Along the Brampton Way

In sun and rain
Ignoring pain
On a cold wet winter's day

Often bikes
And sometimes horses
Join us over river courses

Ducks and pheasants
Rabbits and geese
Are not bothered by us in our fleece

More of us should go and see
What lies around us locally

Gary John Austin

LIFE

Life is just a passage in time,
Ups and downs, and turn arounds.
No money to spend in town.

One day we may sit and watch -
Not the movement of the clock,
But life's simple pleasures.

A dog's nudge, a cat's purr,
A child whispering in your ear.
Walking in the golden autumn leaves.

Awake to the birds at dawn
A brand new day is born.
Treasure these moments
As it it were the last.
These days of life,
Go much too fast!

Sheila Waller

ASHRIDGE

As I strolled amongst the trees
Thinking of times gone by,
A feeling of great contentment
Came into my minds eye.

Remembering when youth
Was too eager to walk,
So one ran and felt free -
No time to talk

What pleasure there was
Just walking along,
Almost in time
To the lovely bird song.

Soft green all around
The arms of the trees
And the bluebells spreading
Their carpets to please

It was good to take
The time to stare
At spring all around
On the ground, in the air
And enjoy all the beauty
Of spring everywhere.

J Harris

SOLITUDE

Oh sweet, gentle peace that soothes the soul
That can restore and make a mind again whole,
It takes away the tortures and rigours
Of daily life that thoughts disfigure.

Oh sweet gentle peace that gives sanity back
You have placed my life again on the right track,
Now the storm and tempest of winter has passed
Spring has come to my life at last.

Shirley Adams

THE MISSING LINK

Pool of pond life,
Swamp of sunlight's pre-Cambrian spawn
Filtering through darkness
Of a world without form.
Stirring cell life
In chance earth's early dawn.
White mist on a silent sea:
Amoeba twitching microbes
Evolve innate wills to be,
Becoming only what they're told -
No hint of what the hour might hold.
And synthesis of sunlight breeds no solace;
Struggling for gain
Against forms without face;
Spreading the gospel
Of its own obdurate race.
Behind the all-consuming eye
A chorus of cold waters cry
'Consume! Consume! Or die!'
What link left food chain
Beyond the skirmishing of cells
To salve survival's strain,
Deeper in the deep?
What spark flamed
From cold earth's keep,
Writhing death throes to feed?
Bleeding for another's need?

Ray Holmes

CHOLESTEROL - THE RIGHT LEVEL:

It's very important for *all* to know
That one's Cholesterol should be 5.2 or below
If it goes above - then be aware
Of the dangers that lurk - if you don't take care.

Learn about HDL; LDL; VLDL;
Be aware of Triglycerides as well
It's very important for *all* to know
That one's Cholesterol should be 5.2 or below

Don't be intimidated by strange sounding words
Taking an interest in one's health is certainly not absurd
Heart attacks and strokes become a diminishing factor
If one's Cholesterol is kept within a safe sector.

Learn about *oatbran* and the protection it can give
To all who practise the desire to live
To live - not exist - is what I urge you to do
Eat *only* what is good for you.

It's not a fad to carefully choose
The foods that nourish - you've *nothing* to lose;
Avoid the fats - they're everywhere
Waiting to clog arteries - so be aware;
Learn about the bad *and* the good
Which exist in every item of food.

Take an interest - be aware
I urge you take the greatest care
For it's *very* important for *all* to know
That one's Cholesterol should be 5.2 or below:

Joan Wilson

SOLITUDE

I never wanted to be alone.
Oh, maybe when I was ten or twelve,
Safe in the arms of mum and dad, I'd say,
'I'll never get married - be some man's slave -
'I'm going to be *me,* take the independent way.

Didn't last long, my dreams of fame -
Only till the end of childhood fantasies.
Than I found grown up love, stronger with each day
And from my childhood home I left to find my own.
Safe again with someone, keeping solitude at bay.

And then came children - filling up my life.
God it's a pain when you want to be alone.
'I'll change my name', I yelled, as day by day
Their childish wants and needs beat round my ears.
'Mum, mum, mum' a thousand times, that's all they say!

But kids grow up and life assumes a gentler pace.
'Thank God I still have you to keep me sane,
'It's too quiet now, with only you and me' I'd say.
You always wanted us to have some time alone
For days and nights - not just an hour or so along the way.

So solitude and I kept well apart
And I was glad I hadn't had my youthful dreams.
You saved me from the lonely, strong, successful way.
How could I know, my love, that you would leave so soon,
While I must stay behind - alone now every day.

Angela Cummins

SEASONS

Time for awakening, that's spring
To something fresh and new
Birds build their nests and start to sing
And all the bulbs come through.

Summer's the time for taking your ease
Cool drinks and shade beneath the trees
But tending the lawns and watering the flowers
Take up so many of your precious hours.

Autumn is quite a busy time
Picking the fruit and making the wine
But leaves are ablaze with red and gold
And mornings and evenings start to grown cold.

Winter's a rest from cutting the grass
Time for hobbies and an evening class
Curtains drawn and fires lit
A good book, and some wool to knit.

Each season has a special pleasure
A bonus, that we cannot measure
So glad and thankful we must be
For blessings given to you and me.

J A Carr

AN INTIMATE COLLISION

An intimate collision
I crashed into her vision,
Her blazing desire
Made my eyes grow wider
And my heart catch fire.

My body lost control
As she bent into my hold
A dark winter's cold
Was released from my soul.
No more was I froze
No more was I alone.

Jason O'Donnell

THE BURGER KING

He's called the Burger King you know, he's only seventeen
A sweaty individual, complete with greasy sheen
His name is Jason Mackintyre, He's 'Big Mac' to his mates
He gives them all free Coke and fries, they go there on their dates

At school he sits right at the back with all his surly friends
Just thinking of that happy time when education ends
For then he dons his uniform, complete with badge and cap
And swaps his ruler and his pen, for burger, chips and bap

A subtle squirt of Mayonnaise, an onion and some dill
some ketchup and some lettuce limp, three fifty at the till
He's cleaned the loos and swept the floor, collected up some trays
Only another seven hours and then he gets his pay

Next week he's Junior Deputy Under-Assistant Boss
It seems that Burgerama's gain is Lloyds of London's loss
He gets an extra special hat, with Burgerama on
A bigger badge, a louder shirt and hook to hang them on!

But now we have to say goodbye, no time to stop and think
Just Quarter Pounder Mega Meal with Regular Fizzy Drink!
He's happy here, he likes the job, the food and everything
He's very good at what he does, He *is* the Burger King!

Bernie King

A WORD

Marriage is the best ingredient of the life
It gives you a partner, a companion a wife

Your days are happy, your nights are fast
Enjoy these times, while they last

Because my friend,
Life after marriage is not all roses
it has many twist, many problems it pauses.

There are times when,
Window closes, programme rolls
Files fade and format falls

Be patient, be considerate, sun shine or rain
Never ever let your system, go down the drain

Best wishes come to you from all your friends
and We hope, your happiness never end.

Finally Ashok, my son
Getting married was the most proper act
which has made you the 'World Perfect'

Afzal Khan Pathan

ON REFLECTION

In '63 our father said,
'Dunstable's the place for us',
We upped our roots and packed our things,
With very little fuss.

We left our rural home back then,
But were very pleased to find,
A railway line, good service too,
And shops of every kind.

18

Lots of jobs, good schools and such -
The envy of our friends,
Not for us a 'One Horse Town,'
With winding lanes and bends.

Now things have changed quite a bit,
And gone the other way,
No railway line, No good jobs,
Shops closing down each day.

The traffic is horrendous,
The fumes could make us ill,
Oh, to be back in the village,
In the peace and fresh air still.

Lynn Parker

DAYDREAM NONSENSE

Just walking through the fields one day
A funny thing came to
What if all the trees were pink
And all the grass was blue.

If all the dogs meowed
And the cats mooed like cows
The hedgehogs gambolled like the lambs
And rabbits were fat - like sows.

What if all the flowers were black
And the birds talked back to you
And if you walked in the snow
Would your feet be covered in dew

What is the sun was a brilliant green
And the clouds a shade of red
That's the thing with daydreaming
Strange thoughts pop in your head

Lyn Keetch

PORTRAIT FOR PEACE

This could be a picture of your dear son,
It could be a likeness of any loved one.
He could be an Arab, he could be a Jew,
He is living and breathing just like you.
His race or religion shouldn't matter a damn,
What really matters is that he's a man.
A brave young man caught up in a cause,
Who suffers the rigours and hardship of wars.
He wants to live in a world that's good,
Not die like a dog in a trench he's dug.
Let's try to resolve all the issues at stake,
And be really sincere in the effort we make.
With his hand on his heart let each man swear,
'I want peace in the land, not that piece of land there.'
Have we learned naught from the wars of the past?
Will Nation speak peace unto Nation at last?
Let us pray for the day when all carnage will cease,
And the whole wide world will live in peace.
Life is too precious for war and for hate,
Will man see the danger - before it's too late?

Eunice Ellis

THE PARTING

O carefree day when all the world was grand!
We made our vows, I offered you my life,
I stood beside you proud to be your wife,
In trust we faced the future hand in hand.

When springtime came we walked along the hill
And in the summer rested by the brook,
My heart was always melted by your look
And as you loved me then, I love you still.

In autumn as the leaves fell from the trees
The fading light, with swirling misty cloud,
Smothered you and wrapped you in a shroud
And carried you away upon the breeze.

And so the winter comes and you are gone
But in my memory springtime lingers on.

Suzanne Davies

FRIEND

What is a friend do you know,
Someone who will never go.
they listen to you when your down,
make you laugh when they act a clown.
Your my friend, my only one.
I've had others, but they don't last long,
but you, you're different from the rest.
You stuck around, stood the test.
We'll be good friends for a long, long time,
to split us up would be a crime
When times are bad you're by my side,
been there for me when I'm cried.
Like the sister I never had,
I know at times I drive you mad.
We have had fights don't get me wrong,
but the arguments don't last for long,
If one of us should move away.
I know as friends we will stay
because we have a special tie
Friendship likes ours will never die.

Tracey Archer

A DAY OF SORROW

Little did I know that morning
What sorrow the day would bring
When a heart of gold stopped beating
And I could not do a thing.

I cannot bring the old days back
When we were all together
But your memory is my greatest treasure
To love, to cherish, and to keep forever.

I wasn't there to see you die
To hold your hand to say goodbye,
But I won't forget my whole life through,
The last few words I had with you,

So look around your garden Lord,
For an angel with a smile,
It won't be hard to find you Deb
For you must stand out a mile

B A Smythe

CHILDHOOD

I can see the little places than mean so much to me,
The winding paths, the hidden ways, the valleys and the streams.
I can see the little rabbits ever watchful yet serene,
I can see the shadows of the evening spreading o'er the lovely scene.
I can hear the strangest echoes, the whistles and the barks,
The sounds, ah so familiar, in the stillness of the dark.
I can hear those lilting voices, they take me in their pitch,
To a scene that I have painted with images so rich.

I can feel the rain so gently falling, the wind blowing through the trees,
The crows and seagulls squawking as they struggle in the breeze.
I can smell the scent of bogland and the whiff of new-mown hay,
The delightful smell of dinner in the middle of the day.
I can feel the warmth in my heart for nature pulls the strings
For the far off days of childhood and nature's simple things.

Frank Horan

PURE WHITE DOVE

When I see you dancing high up there,
I get confused, trying not to despair.
Because you have such freedom in that tranquil air.
Soaring up further, making me weep,
Every mile you take I find incredibly steep.
You're free so incredibly free,
You're that pure white dove that passionately influences me,
Down here I am gagged and bound,
Bound by the woes of mankind,
Chained by the noise of a modern world,
Crying out for a comforting hand.
You are my air, you are my sky,
You are my nectar, without you I'd die.

Olivia Brown

LOVE

Love, defies the boundaries
Of all the laws of life.
Its strength and passion strong enough
To overcome all strife,
The deep emotional feelings,
For those we dearly love,
That dwell within our very soul,
Are sent from Heaven above.
A warm embrace, a tender smile,
A caring word that's spoken,
The gentle touch of a loving hand
And vows that are unbroken.
The power of love can beat all hate,
All envy, and all sneers,
For it alone, can soothe the mind
In sadness, and in tears.
It guards those precious moments,
That's secret in your heart,
And turns them into memories
Forever to impart
And as you journey on life's way,
Give thanks to God above,
For all the gifts He gave to you
Faith, Hope, but most of all, for love.
The heart controls the destiny
Of what we do and say.
But love, alone can give it strength,
No matter, come what may.
Time cannot change a faithful heart,
Though weary it may be.
But love, will be there to the end,
And in Eternity.

Francis Whittemore

A CHRISTIAN FRIEND

O Barry so tall and so great
so many paths you must take
the path's for people who are
lost and found will find you
upon the righteous ground.

Peter Weed

THE KEY

I've got the key to a secret,
A secret I can't let out,
The secret's hidden inside me,
The secret's trying to get out,
I know I'd feel much better,
If I told mum or dad,
But this might cause aggravation,
And I really don't want that.
I've thought it through very carefully,
I've cried night after night,
It's been playing on my mind,
And now I've come to the end of my fight.
I felt so stupid, just if I'd told,
I wouldn't be here now,
It just came spilling out one day,
I thought my parents would go mad,
But no instead they listened,
I guess I found the key,
The key to the secret,
The secret I no longer have.

Nicola Walker (14)

BLIND DATE

I once met a charming optician
and exchanged some strange inhibitions
he tested my eyes,
whilst looking for lies,
and gave me a whole new prescription.

We discussed in some depth my perspective,
and he told me of methods corrective,
when sensing my vision
he reached the decision
that glasses would be ineffective.

His manner was gentle and soothing,
as he assured me my sight was improving,
but I still could not see
the reason why we
found the alphabet quite so confusing.

Convinced that my case was not hopeless,
he worked with renewed sense of purpose,
until the previously blurred
four-letter word
gradually came into focus.

He suggested we try to refract,
said myopia would not detract,
and a clear twenty-twenty
was quite elementary
when we managed to see all the facts.

Tracy Coles

A THOUGHT FOR THE DAY

The comfort and pleasure we get from a friend
The satisfaction of sharing our all,
Is just as rewarding you'll agree in the end
And you'll find that you feel six feet tall.

The things that we do and the things that we say,
Affect our whole way of life.
For all the promotions that happen each day
Can cause us contentment or strife

So take what you have and be grateful
There are those who would like what you've got
Be gracious and kind, don't be hateful
And be satisfied with your lot.

Laurie Barnes

ASH

Not long to go
People crying softly so
Crying into the burning winds around their head
Weeping for a world that is nearly dead
Time of innocence gone away
One act of hate the world's gone today,
Dream on of regret through tears of pain
Ever nearer just things of ash remain
Sleep now people that dreamless sleep
On the ground that your body will forever keep.
Lifeless and still, nothing grows or renews
All murdered and gone because of political views.
Too late to change it, the deed is done
Does it matter now which side has won . . .

A C Stock

SONG OF A DIY VICTIM

I've had a hard day's work,
The Everest of stairs grows as I climb.
My head, shoulders and feet ache,
and there's a wardrobe in the bathroom.

I'll have a cup of tea,
Two sugars and a biscuit,
Clear my headache, battle with the stairs,
There's still a wardrobe in the bathroom.

My wife's in a cupboard,
The children are watching Neighbours.
Maybe my headache hasn't gone after all.
Why is there a wardrobe in the bathroom?

I've watched the news and weather twice,
Eaten dinner and made a bonfire,
But I can't wash my hands
Because there's a wardrobe in the bathroom.

Oh good, the kids have moved it,
I can go and have a bath.
I conquer the stairs again but what do I find?
There's a wardrobe on the landing.

Jennie Pollock

THE HERBIVORE

The masses believe that we're quite a strange lot,
Like wanting to eat green lentil hot pot,
The bare reality is quite the reverse,
Why eat an animal? It's quite perverse.
I see no difference in consuming a pet,
Would you eat your dog? Not even for a bet?

Some have us labelled hippies or loons,
For trying to stop the use of harpoons,
But 'Ah' you say, 'we don't eat whales,'
Please tell Japan and stop their sales,
For even countries with a few morals intact,
Find it hard to boast culling as a necessary fact.

We don't all live in tents, tepees or huts,
To stand against convention does take a lot of guts,
But some of us prefer a more gentle action,
Without summoning the wrath of warring factions,
To lead our protest by refusing to eat,
The blood of an undercooked slab of meat.

S Nash

ONE MAY MORNING IN THE GARDEN

I could see some trees being
pushed by the breeze;
I could see some daisies and
then some bees.
I could hear some birds singing
their song;
I could hear the bells ringing,
Ding-dong!
I could smell the flowers like
tall coloured towers,
And I could feel the air in my
long golden hair!

Katy Kettleborough

THE LIGHT OF THE MOON

By the light of the moon she glistened,
Her body bathed in unearthly glow.
As the waves met the beach she listened,
To the voice of the sea far below.

By the light of the moon she hovered,
On the cliff by the sand of the shore.
In life with her no-one has bothered,
To see that she finds it a chore.

By the light of the moon she debated,
On life and its harrowing theme,
And the feeling inside that is hatred.
The feeling that led to this scheme.

By the light of the moon I saw her.
Tearful eyes they beckoned the sky.
By the light of the moon her torture,
Was ended she leapt with a cry.

R Harrington

THE GARDEN

I walked into a garden
And what a sight I saw
A multitude of colours
Lay like a carpet on the floor.

A trellis full of roses
Tended with great care.
The sweet smell of honeysuckle.
Perfume filled the air.

The pansies and the bluebells
Gave an ocean of display.
Daffodils stood, their heads were tall.
Anemones woke in the day.

My eyes can't see the beauty
Of this garden as I'm blind.
But while I can smell the flowers.
There's a garden in my mind.

Trudie Cockle

LONELINESS

Strange and unexpected emotions
raged, unguided through her innermost.
Taking her to a wilderness.
Lost amid confusion, with no hope of true guidance -

The sharp icy feelings, cut into her tearful heart.
Devotion and loyalty was coming to an end.

Bleak forlorn energy, that was once solid and true,
lay battered and naked.
Surrounding mists, echoed their promises, in a profound
conspiracy.

This weak and feeble wreck, unsure and desperate for belief,
drifted aimlessly, alone and vulnerable.
She'd shown signs of holding together,
But disturbed by all the silences,
she drifted and was washed away.

Jane McMaken

CYNICAL VIBES - A BLACK PROSPECTIVE

Our streets are paved with gold they said
so we let it go right to our heads
and believed the words that brought us here
but since discovered insincere.

Come and bring your family too
we're here to take good care of you
no need to worry of where to stay
no-one here will turn you away

There is enough for all to share
in this community we care
you're black we know and that's no blight
you're human too so it's your right.

Those optimistic days have past
the euphoric fever didn't last
like those that promised us and lied
our plans and dreams have long since died

So we work and strive for better things
but don't know what the future brings
we dream of lands our fathers fled
cause our streets are paved with gold they said.

Vincent Raymond

DOWN THE LANE

In a field just down the lane
I go there time and time again
At the peaceful view I stand and gaze
And watch the cows as they graze

I see the hedgerows and trees so tall
A scene so beautiful to us all
At the gate to meadows green
I see the buttercups all serene

I take my stroll into the past
For it seems to me I have found at last
A haven of tranquillity
Just down the lane for all to see

I hope and pray that blessed I'll be
This wondrous view through life I'll see
And till I die in mind I'll keep
This peaceful view to lull me to sleep.

George Emery

SPRING

Evening sunlight simpers.
Spring stretches its lips.
Fresh spots feel my fingers.
Excess sap drips
From a fresh-cut sapling
In the thickening hedge.
Decibels are widening
Driving in their wedge,
Creating new sight,
Changing the light
To kaleidoscopes of pop.
Sudden smooth legs,
Curving shoulders,
Sprout inevitably
From hidden hot trunks
Whose revealed cleavage
Keeps its inward secret,
Rousing and hiding,
Suggesting, denying,
A perpetual, short-lived dance.

Ali Cohen

NORTHERN TRUTH

I want to die a soldier's death
in remembrance be hailed a hero
the excuse found in bravery
just cause for an empty promise.
Embroidered in fear, quarantined from peace
entrusted with a weapon to reject or protect
with no guidelines of conduct
no measurement of guilt

Assured conviction to stay mute and balanced
fully resolute in self-motivation
the stance is the strength
to imitate duty, bound in loyalty
by rights to fight without passion or prejudice
the desire for automated response
in ignorance the longing to live
in other's arms to be held in peace secured.

What way of reason can bypass
the invested pitfalls and tested paths?
Though in hungry dreams
the mocking moonlight still casts its scorn.

In force the resolute voice
commands to stand or fall.
the once enriched souls now
in mirrored darkness they haunt.

I want to die a free man's death.
In remembrance become forgotten.
The excuse found in honest fear,
just cause for freedom's promise.

Joseph P Quinn

QUIET THOUGHTS

A quietness surrounds us while we wait
as one year ends, another's journey is about to begin,
yesterday now must fade from view
for the ticking clock cannot be stilled.
Alone each man wanders in his own thoughts,
thinking how soon his life was but - passing time,
faces emerge as memories come flooding back
remembering the days of laughter, days of youth,
fears and doubts unsure which path to choose,
stumbling around with a haunted look.

Such sobering thoughts, spectres not always stilled,
by the touch of a gentle hand,
Shutting out the sadness which touched our souls
the void which never leaves,
the kindness shown - but never fills
when those you love have gone before,
loneliness comes with the closing of a door
Frightened and fearful what the future holds
some do fall on the precarious rocks,
loss of faith begins to stir - is anyone there?
each one hoping as the sun does rise,
All have known these traumas along the way,
then guidance comes bringing wisdom in its wake,
watching it all - from age old time
it's our destiny who calls us.
As the minutes rush past, pushing each into eras new
we sit in silence, for the clock to chime.

H J

A CHRISTMAS WISH

What new words can I say
About the magic of Christmas Day,
My favourite time of the year.
The day put aside to celebrate the birth of a boy
Who was to change the ways of the world and bring such joy.

It's supposed to be the time of peace and goodwill toward all men,
Why is it then
That many go hungry, or die in some senseless war,
And many, many people go poor.
Why can't there be a Christmas law
Stating everyone gets plenty to eat,
And those who usually go cold have enough heat.
Let all men shake hands that day
Then let us all pray
That it continues that way.

I know it would need a miracle for all this,
But wouldn't it be such bliss
For there to be no more hunger or war,
No poverty, no animals slain
For those humans who are so vain.

Why can't people of this cruel world change their way
And when better to start than on Christmas Day.

Lesley Stevenson

ONE DAY IN MY LIFE

One day in my life I saw
One hundred horses pulling forth a golden chariot across the evening sky,
Followed by one thousand soldiers silhouetted against the glow
The orange dust melting them away as the light faded.

I waited all night hoping they would return.
Hour by hour I waited under the stars.
Then in the distance I saw a glow; night heralded day
As one hundred horses pulling forth a golden chariot returned.
Brighter and brighter the sky became until I could see no more
But not one soldier returned.

Rod Stalham

ALONE

Deep inside a stirring an ache,
A feeling, an emotion
A dream withering
somewhere in my soul
a dream alone . . .

Seeking, searching
holding on
A feeling of pain that forever grows,
May I rest?
Will the search never end?

A facade
Masquerading,
Hiding
Would I really want to know?
Hidden are the visions
deeply in my soul.

Let me know the secrets you hold,
Bring out the life in this empty soul
The feeling, the fervour -
cannot fold
Or let is sleep
Be empty, alone.

Maxine Walton

ALL IS WELL

The day comes quickly but the years come long
And briefly, for one moment, I will steal you from Eternity,
And hold your phantom hand in mine
To tell you all is well.
Gone now the grey-black loneliness
That played companion with me everywhere,
It tucked me up in bed at night
Then came to breakfast;
When visiting for tea it came with me
Squeezing itself beside me in the chair
Then raced me home
And waited in the keyhole like a mischievous imp.

But Time glides gently over grief
And memory swings from Life to Death
And Death to Life again to tell you All is Well.

Ru Seymour

A LETTER FROM A FRIEND

A letter means more to me
than a telephone conversation.
A letter to treasure, I can keep
and re-read at my leisure.
Secrets shared on paper,
jokes to make me laugh.
Gossip from another town,
tales of another part.
All the news that can be told
until comes writers' cramp.
A two way conversation
all for the price of a stamp.

Maggie Prickett

TRUE BEAUTY

True beauty is not held within your face,
It's found within a much more secret place.

True beauty is hidden inside your soul.
It hides inside a deep dark hole.

True beauty can glow out of your eyes.
Its presence takes you by surprise.

It's found within the kindest heart.
And in true beauty love has got a part.

You might be stirred by a beautiful face.
But always remember true beauty's place.

Jackie Culley

CHILDHOOD THOUGHTS

We as children always see the world as a rosy place,
All the things we look upon transform beneath our gaze.

What colours we spy as Spring arrives and all is bright and fair,
Our eyes go bright with wonder at sunlight on our hair.

And then the feel of Autumn the wind upon our face,
The leaves and berries around us growing in every place.

And then the cold of winter the warmth within us grows,
Maybe we still are children just waiting for the snow.

M Lord

39

WORDS

What pain in words;
Sharper than swords they come
Tearing, destroying trust,
Twisting, each word a sharp-edged tooth,
Lies - twisted, turned,
To become the truth.

They hurt, those words,
Sicken and destroy,
Ugly sounds; daggers poised
Like poisoned spears,
Gold turned to Love's alloy.

'Sticks and stones . . .'
So goes the rhyme,
Ah, but cuts and bruises heal,
The words you mean to harm
Just leave an empty heart,
Like an empty sleeve
On an amputated arm.

Rita Hayter Cullen

OUR OWN BIT OF HEAVEN

We can all have our own bit of heaven out there.
We must take it with both hands, because it is rare.
There are those whom we love, we must treasure each hour,
Because love can turn to hate, and all things turn sour.
We must keep putting something back or we exhaust our own supply,
Don't keep looking backwards, it stops us from aiming too high.
Take pleasure from nature's free things in life,
Make life a pleasure, not a constant strife.
Just be there for each other, see another's point of view.
Then perhaps you'll be treated with love and respect too.

Sylvia Holdstock

EGO-CHAOS

Dissect my shattered ego
Into diamond fragments,
Rhyming the harmonious chords
Into a bright mosaic of sound.

Displace the debris of broken strings
Into the oblivion of an uplifting sonata,
Now let me hear my contented symphony
In harmony with yours!

Elizabeth Anne Beale

THE OLD CITY

Unlit back streets, darkened rooms,
Flowers wilting, falling blooms,
Ancient churches, discoloured stones,
Harbours for discarded bones,
Once proud buildings stand, disused,
Their roofs, and windows torn abused,
Wondrous theatres of bygone days,
Spoiled in oh! so many ways,
Once upon its stage such treats,
Now just empty bingo seats,
Tin factories belch and billow smoke
Its inhabitants to slowly choke,
Yet in this city, drear and dark,
Between squashed houses, a lush green park,
Where roses grow, and air smells sweet,
And the patter of such tiny feet,
Where people walk at end of day,
Between green trees, that swish and sway,
I'm sure their thoughts drift back in time,
To mental pictures of a long past prime.

Syn

YOUR PILLOW

Oh how I wish I was your pillow
To be there when you sleep,
Cradle your sweet head below
Within your dreams I'd creep.
First eyes in daylight early
Before the world was conscious,
To kiss, a love, so dearly,
As morning fell upon us.
Yet in the day commitment strain
Our yearning hearts would long,
And weaken till we meet again,
Recharged with love so strong.
How deep we are where helpless lies,
Stood still, on a merry-go-round,
Clear crystal, fountain eyes,
Still blinding, portraying all we found.
Forever young in heart and mind
My memories, deep, not shallow,
And when I leave this world behind.
I'll wish I was your pillow.

John Gilbert Conning

MY PRAYER FOR YOU

May there be fluttering of Angels' wings
O'er the place where you're lying
May you hear their gentle voices
Murmuring and sighing.
May there be soft clouds over you
Fanned by a gentle breeze
Oh yes, I most sincerely wish you
All of these.

May all your requests be granted
According to your will
May you lie peacefully
And all the night be still
May you wake tenderly to see
The dawn wind in the trees
Oh yes, I most sincerely wish you
All of these.

Grace Cameron-Pratt

ATLAS, HOPE AND LOST

This dwelling holds three souls, all different and unique.
Who share each other's lives every day of every week.

One soul carries the weight of the world on her shoulders,
we shall call her Atlas.

The second is young and excitable, her name is Hope
which is doubtless.

I'm the last who feels lost.

Atlas' moaning always has its cost. She expects every soul
to pick up the fragments of her broken peace of mind,
but after a while, the reasons to help her become not so kind.

Hope is happy and tries to think of the best,
this soul always provides Lost's heavy heart with a rest.

Lost feels content in life,
apart from Atlas' moaning which causes strife.

She knows everyone's soul is unique in the world,
but sometimes she wishes her feelings could be unfurled.

C Holme

WHEN I WAS YOUNG

When I was young the spring was conjured at command.
the autumn and the winter - death of love -
were not for me;
when the sun sank on evenings of dull pain
I'd walk and walk away,
knowing it would rise again.

I left you then,
hearing you say 'remember when . . .'
for something and some time we shared together.

it was not you I loved so much
as shooting stars
and gentle murmuring Sunday afternoons.

Until
there was no-one to love
no-one to leave

and all the flowers were dying.

Michael J Browne

A HAPPY DAY

The trees swayed gently from side to side
As down the Avenue came the Bride.
Looking radiant, all dressed in white
She looked to everyone, a most beautiful sight.

The carriage with her white horses
Her father and Her, did ride
He was always so proud of his Daughter
And today, he had her by his side.

They Both made a lovely picture
Everyone came out, and waved their hand
We wish Her, and her new Husband, a long life together
As they are going to live, in another Land.

Elizabeth Ann Collis

SAMUEL AND ALEXANDRA

You taste your first orange
A bright, wet segment
Spilling juice on your little fingers
How I laugh as you wince!
I remember the sharpness.
Alex
You are my hope and my future
The prodigy that I'm not
I love to touch your hair
Brown, like mine.

Your sister is noisy, Sam.
Her laughter wakens you
Her anger frightens you
Her love surrounds you.
A little man already, you have
Podgy feet, pink ears
But girls' eyes
Lashed thick with black bristles
Your surprised blink
And your dimpled elbows
Delight me

I wish you wisdom,
Brother, sister.

Lauren J Harris

OTHER PEOPLE'S FAILINGS

Why is it I so easily recognise
Faults in others that Society despise
I believe I have a heightened sense
As if the lack has been recompensed
Some I concede I have in mild measure
Which I consider to be simple pleasures
As would others who are well versed
In human failing, that are far worse
They are of the pontificating type
And lecture to the sinful and the like
As some clergymen with whom I am acquainted
Through abstinence could lay my claim to be sainted

Brian Norman

GARDEN IN THE SKY

There is a garden in the sky,
where flowers bloom,
they grow so high,
Each one a life that's been and gone,
but in these flowers, souls live on.

There is a wind that gently blows,
to tell us it's our time to go,
How soft the breeze that takes us there,
Safely held by hands of air.

And in this peaceful sleep you'll stay,
for *them* it's just another day,
and though warm teardrops they may cry,
the flowers live, they'll never die.

Stephanie Hall

46

LETTING GO

I look at all the mums here
Outside the big school gates
Smiles and elation at
What the letter states.

Why are they all so happy?
at the news we've just received
when I feel so sad, so solemn,
heartbroken and grieved.

The letter says they start full-time
when they return next term
A whole long day when every minute
for my daughter I will yearn.

They laugh and say 'Why the long face?
It's not so bad you'll see.'
It's all too easy for them to scorn,
When it's the youngest of their three.

But she's my eldest, the first to leave
my first pure bundle of joy
So sweet and innocent
and so very coy.

I know I've got to let her go
from underneath my wing
To discover there's another world
which she has a place in.

So I'll bite my lip, allay my tears
and take her to the class
And just count each and every minute
For that first day to pass.

Jennifer Ann Reid

LIGHT FROM DARK

The years of tender, bitter days
Our laughter shared, our special ways.
Do you really care for the loving heart,
I was lost to yours right from the start.

A boy, a girl, a mum and dad,
A unity we all once had.
Can we ever have the same as then,
The years are ours, they count to ten.

Try to take aboard all the pain I've felt,
Feel I've been shut out, crazy cards I've been dealt.
Just can't walk this path, by my very own,
Seeds of love for you, have long been sown.

Can't protect you all, from the dark surrounds,
Shall we play no more, are we out of bounds.
Help us all, I pray, must my heart despair,
Have no chance to show, how I really care.

Please remember us, just recall the days,
All the things we've loved, they're not faint remains.
In our heart they'll stay, it's the truth you know,
Bide our time and wait, light from dark might show.

Mark Turney

SNOW'S BEAUTY

Silently the snowflakes fall
To change a familiar view
It comes across and settles down
As quiet as morning dew

It covers all the barren earth
It gives a bed of white
In winter time where it is dark
It makes the landscape light

What patterns on each bush and tree
The tiny snowflakes make
Each one different to the rest
Like mountain, stream and lake

They are a wonder to behold
Like hawthorn frost that lasts
A few short minutes, then it's gone
A new die has been cast

Mary Aris

UNTITLED

The chestnuts down the avenue
Just one look from me to you
I saw your grace, I saw your smile
I knew you'd be here for a while
I look, watch, see and stare
How do I tell you I care
We'll walk for hours in the park
Until the light has turned to dark
A chance for us, for you and me
A chance for us, to be free.

A Greenacre

RIVER SEASON

Bedford in Summer, her trees are ever green,
The clouds loiter above the calming trees.
Far off in the distant a lawn-mower starts its job.
Then a dragonfly comes
To the shimmering river.
The trees in lazy June,
make tents of dim shiny light.
Sunlight weaves in their leaves
The wind blows gently at the trees.
Through the heavy heat of the summer's air.
Children sing, play and laugh,
The river has come alive.

Bedford in Winter, her trees have no heads,
The river's only sound, her banks a sudden stop.
Halfway up the bridge, a ghost of a man,
glances at me and then disappears.
The distant fog has spirited him away.
I cannot see my hand before my face,
My body does not seem to be my own.
Bedford becomes a far-off foreign place.
People are strangers, houses silent.
The river is unknown.

Carol Gilby

TIME TRAVELLERS

I am I, not mother, daughter, wife or widow,
Someone with inner sorrows, tears and doubts,
I have many troubles which surface in my mind,
And all unheard, not wanting to be shared.
I have much joy in the beauty of this earth,
Sadness for necessity of ugliness and pain.

And you are you, so different, yet the same,
Instinctively I know the words you cannot say,
Feel the loneliness and fears you do not show,
But life goes on, and we must enter and depart,
For you must realise and sense as well as I,
Together or alone, we are travellers in time.

Elizabeth Shorley

A PURPOSE FOR MY BEING

To know that I am special,
Truly one of a kind.
A man born to make a difference,
So sure in my own mind.

A wondrous revelation,
A gift adorned to me,
A purpose for my being,
For everyone to see.

The one thing that will happen,
Be it large or small,
My personal own achievement,
There for one and all.

But I am still waiting,
Still searching for my goal,
Something truly different,
Or an ointment for my soul.

Still onward as I travel,
Just waiting for my day,
The greatness that is owing,
Is bound to come my way.

Neil Carn

WHY?

Sometimes I sit and wonder
Why the world is as it is
With war and fear and hunger
and poor homeless families
Why is there so much badness
and cruelty and deceit
Why is it that we fight
and steal and do bad things and cheat.
Why can't the world be as one,
full of laughter and of glee,
and then what a much happier place
this world of ours would be.

April Woodworth

EGG SHELLS

When we tread hard upon the ground
Egg shells break with a crunching sound
When softly our steps we take
Shells stay whole and do not break
We all walk upon egg shells
And how we tread through life tells
When hard we walk through life span
Breaking and hurting we do of man
But if we take great care and thought
Happiness, love and peace we have brought

Gilian Bichard

AT THE GATE

Balanced on a knife edge,
Looking back I see the dark.
Far below existence beckons;
Seductive, I know the world is deadly.
Now I must place one foot forward.
How can I prevent a fall?
Directly to the light ahead;
Tightly, with no wavering.
Calmly I must not fall down.
Maybe I will make the leap,
Grace will transfigure me;
Knightly with a shining lance,
Running to my latest fate.

M Blewett

WHY

Why do you tell me what to do
And what I have to wear?
Why do you tell me what I should say
And how I must have my hair?

Why do you get mad with me
When I don't get mad with you?
It's not my fault that you're grown up
And I am only two!

Carol Ann James

CONCRETE

Yesterday it rained
all afternoon
all evening
all night
spilling acid
drop after drop
on homebound
gutless urchins
boozers
back-street cruisers
while the user-losers
sleep.
Seep after seep
of corrosion
has rivered its way
even into our
script
ripping us apart.
Now the concrete is covered
by leaves
our stone still grave.

K Hudson

UNTITLED

G od's garden is a beautiful place.
L et's sit a while, and contemplate.
A heady perfume fills the air.
D reams of yesterday are there.
Y our memories in the heart to stay.
S hall never forget this peaceful day.

Irene Corin

THAT'S LIFE

I remember in my childhood, and in my early teens,
Life was full of hope and love and of lovely dreams,
I dreamt of falling in love and being happy evermore,
But those dreams soon went out of the door,
I thought if I got married, and became somebody's wife,
I'd be happy evermore for the rest of my life,
But now that I am older I know it's all a joke,
Life is not a bit like that, it's just a great big hoax,
So all you young people with your hopes and dreams of love,
Just make the most of what you've got and thank God above,
Because when you get older, you'll discover just like me,
That whatever is going to happen whatever will be, will be,
Life goes by as quickly as a wink,
You'll soon be old yourself much sooner than you think.

F V Tubb

AFTER DARK

The dawn is breaking, it's after dark,
The birds are awake, the occasional bark,
Disturbs the quiet, from the unreal peace,
The streets are quite empty, but that will soon cease,
There's a strange kind of beauty at this time of day,
The roads all seem clean, with the cars all at bay,
The smell of the dew, seems so fresh on the grass,
The song of the birds, does it soon have to pass,
Just look at the doves, high up on that steeple,
Why welcome the sun, when it brings out the people.

Sandy Fryer

55

THE BLUEBELL WOODS

Out walking with the dog on
a cold January day, though
the sun was shining brightly
the wind still had its way

Fields all around in sombre hue
activity taking place underground
hidden from our view, but teeming
with life which abounds

Birds darting through trees
searching for winter food,
beneath the brambles, the foxes
earth waiting for night to come

Despite recent frost and winter snow
touches of spring are starting to show,
buds on branches bursting through
snowdrops and daffodils peeping out too.

The thought that spring is on its way
warms your heart on a winter's day.
I turn for home and a cosy fire
a cup of tea my heart's desire

L Burton

FAMINE

I am Famine,
I strike any time,
I take all your food and animals,
One at a time.

I am Famine,
I can't be seen.
I will come and go,
Until you've got nothing - but a bean.

I am Famine,
I am like a disease,
Once I have spread,
I'll take all I please.

Alan Doerr (12)

MYSTERY MAN

Unknown figure, sighted across the park
Usual time, always just before dark
Whistling tunes beckoning the mutt
Nearing return, before the gates are shut

Friendly wave, cheery hello
High on a hill, me just below
Frisky canine, meeting mine
Stay a little longer, just this time

Apart from a greeting, no other words spoken
But deep inside, something wonderful has woken
Wondering about this handsome man
So innocent to my devious plan

Planning a coincidence of meeting him
Memorising the words with a winning grin
Dressed to attract, with best attire
Hoping my look will promptly aspire

Next time maybe we will walk
Get to know each other with simple talk
Lift the barriers, remove the shield
Of my mystery man from across the field.

Jane C Cook

THE COTTAGE GARDEN

Just past the church and down the lane
a quaint old cottage stands.
The flowers in the garden there
massed colours they are grand.

The path that leads up from the gate
past hollyhocks so tall.
And past delphiniums spiky blue
sunflowers by the wall.

The arch with honeysuckle there
is such a pretty sight.
Its perfume brings the fragrance
that lingers in the night.

Geraniums, pinks and marigold
large peonies red and white.
Deep purple blue the lavender
lobelia sparkling bright.

Clematis up the trellis
just see how fast it grows.
Pale yellow pink with many flowers
they call Montana Rose.

The foxgloves, daisies, marguerites
and dahlias in the sun.
Azaleas in their coloured bush
outshone by only one.

The climbing roses year by year
their beauty proudly bear.
Soft colours fragrance and delight
the *English Rose* so fair.

Alan J Vincent

MY PERFECT WORLD

Shimmering reflections brightly glow, evolving the calm
tranquil stream, into a flowing liquid of gold.
A smell of sweet aromas float by on a warm gentle
breeze, then vanish without trace, into this place so
wise and so old.

Keeping its secrets wrapped up, within an eerie
swirling early mist of a tepid summer morn.
While in the heights and the sanctuary of eternally
watchful trees, birds chirp seemingly meaningful ballads of dawn.

Bouffant clouds glide lazily by, set against the
infinite blue of a motionless sky.
Occasionally, shedding pure droplets of crystal clear rain,
that are discarded to earth when the angels do cry.
A food of great value, and a giver of life, enabling young
flowers of great beauty to flourish and grow.
Sharp blades of green grass, arc gently and entwine,
into a tapestry of life swaying steady and slow.

This magical kingdom of plentiful life, must have been
blessed with a kiss by our Lord from above.
A feeling of peace was then spread to every far
reaching corner, when He opened His hand, and set free, a
silken white dove.
Such an ideal setting, within an ideal world, absolutely
perfect in every way it would seem.
But alas, this wonderful place is entirely my own, and
its existence lives deep in my mind and my dreams.

P T Mead

CHILDHOOD

Carefree, happy, innocent, that was me,
With hopes, ambitions, I was young, I was free.
You always miss things that have passed,
God, why did I try and grow up too fast?
I look back and can't remember the day,
that my childhood fell and slipped away.

I think too much,
about what I don't understand.
I try and make light of ideas,
and grasp them in my hand.

Memories are like shadows,
spinning round in a confused mind
I have no events,
Just images which I can't find.

The world's on my doorstep,
Well, I don't want to step outside,
The pen and paper is how I choose to confide.

My infancy was a happy one, I was secure and loved,
That's why I miss it so much.

Michelle Harding

THE MAGIC OF FLOWERS

When I look upon flowers
What do I see?
Beautiful faces
Looking at me.

Soft gentle rosebuds
or a full mixed bouquet
Large heads or small heads
they all have their say.

60

The shapes of the petals
the smell of the scent.
Wonderful colours
all Heaven lent.

Nothing can cheer me
like the pleasures they give
Flowers - my one love
for as long as I live.

J D Swain

NEW LIFE

The age of innocence
so gentle and pure,
closed to the ways of the world,
so naive and unsure.

So soft so new
unable to speak your mind
you have to rely on your mother's loving care
and anyone else's you may find.

You're just a baby
beautiful to the touch,
a tiny human being
who needs love so much.

As you travel through life
many obstacles you will face,
and you will need the strength to cope with
each change that takes place.

I M Godbold

THE BIRD TABLE

When wintry winds do blow
And the snow is on the ground,
The birds are cold and hungry
For there is nothing to be found.

So fill up the bird table
With bread and bacon rind,
Apple, nuts and biscuit
And scraps of every kind.

The guests will soon come flocking
To this very welcome feast,
From cocky, noisy starling
Down to robin, not the least.

A flock of gossiping sparrows
With a flutter will descend,
The thrush and then the blackbird
On our thoughtfulness depend.

And there upon the washing line
A bag of nuts we'll fix,
Where the greenfinches and titmice
Will do their acrobatic tricks.

And later on when Spring arrives
And Winter's gone away,
How glad we'll be to hear the birds
A-singing through the day.

Ruth Purdy

HOME

I've been wandering for so long,
So many miles, so many songs,
Just take me home.
I've been wandering for so long,
Take me home to where I belong.
When it comes down to it all
There's a life out there
And it seems so small,
Until you look into its face
With your back against the wall.
I've been travelling oh so long
I don't know where I started from.
Take me home to where I belong.
Safe from the world outside in here,
Take me home.

Henry Harding

BLOOD AND TEARS

Why do they shed blood
To cause tears to flood
Why do they destroy homes
What of the people becomes
Misery and grief
Giving no relief
All because of greed
Leaving millions with no feed
More land they want
What is the point
Can not they live in peace
And let life have a longer lease.

Malcolm W Davison

ODE TO LEIGHTON BUZZARD

Oh Leighton Buzzard, grey are your roads, buildings and skies,
You don't seem so very attractive to passers by,
The High Street's becoming a ghost town bit by bit,
The Bossard centre's old and run down and people are getting sick of it.

We are bombarded by agents of travel and estate,
And as another shop closes down, we know that space's fate,
It shall be filled with yet another charity shop's array,
When will our local people get a say?

A visitor can fill up with petrol every two metres down road,
And as Safeway's petrol station is built, good it doesn't bode,
Our roads are jammed and congested, traffic lights abound,
What was the point of our bypass because still they don't go around?

Our local news is full of gloom, crime and violence,
When will our local graffiti artists be stamped out to silence?
Each night teenagers violate the market cross,
When will our youth be entertained, so they're no longer at a loss?

But what does our town have to offer our people?
It has a historic market place and All Saints with its steeple,
There's the canal with painted barges and an old steam railway,
And if things really get bad, there's the trains to whisk you away.

A E Fox

FOR JANICE

Is love contained in the sweetest kiss?
Or in the merest touch of hands?
When beating heart oft goes amiss,
Is this all that love demands?

Was love ever meant to last?
Could this be the mould of a million lives?
Still gleaming through the ages past
Could love, an ageing soul revive?

Yet, for all my faults you love me still,
Imperfect though I seem to be.
And you, in turn, indeed fulfil
All that is best in charity.

For love in all its rapturous scope
Inspires low men with lofted hopes.

P H Schoon

AMNESIA

Strangers' pictures on the walls,
Unknown faces stop to call
       Awoken in a coma
       living in a dream
       Who am I?
       Where have I been?
Memory empty, mind a blank
Waiting for a ship - already sank
       Name: Jane Doe
       Address: Unknown
       Who am I?
       What have I done?

Gemma Johnson

PLOUGHMAN'S POEM

As I look out of my window,
An old man I see,
Wearing a cloak,
Worn and poor,
With no shoes upon his feet.

As I look out to a field,
I see the man working,
Over the plough bending,
Worn and poor,
With no shoes upon his feet.

As I look out to the distance,
His family I see,
A wife and two children,
Worn and poor,
With no shoes upon their feet.

As I look out to the mists,
I remember the place,
Where the ploughman once stood,
Worn and poor,
With no shoes upon his feet.

Fiona Tulloch (12)

MEMORIES

The pictures in the album
Might make you shed some tears,
As you look back with memory
Of all those happy years.

Sweet memories will please you
As you see those photographs,
The times that you remember
Will cause you many laughs.

But never will those days return
So this is what I'll say
'Be happy love forever more
Remembering today.'

Look forward to tomorrow,
Don't look back my friend,
For life goes on from day to day
Until the very end.

Theresa Rhodes

AUTUMN PROMISES

It's afternoon in autumn time,
The leaves are fiery red,
And golden brown and yellow now,
With promises to shed.

The woods are bare and silent here
And autumn makes me weep
But autumn's kiss is seasonal,
With promises to keep.

The carpet crunches noisily,
Under paws and feet,
And promises a warm dry bed,
To harbour winter sleep.

It covers up and nourishes,
Nuts and seeds, with hopes to grow,
And promises ripe berries who,
Will feed the ones who know

But autumn's chill makes promises
To many old and weak,
Of winter's cold deliverance,
Of honest endless sleep.

Sue Jacob

WOMAN

Woman is deep.
Mystical.
Woman bears the fruit of the tree of life,
from within her pours forth a fountain,
nurtures the child of her breast.
The future.

The wellspring of wisdom,
flows from Mother to daughter,
from Time until now.

She beholds all sorrow in her eyes,
as she looks upon the Earth.
Mankind destroys all Woman stands for,
Life.

Woman is strong, Love, solid as the mountain,
Beautiful as the wind
Abundant as the World.

Lucy Rix

PRECIOUS LOVE

How many ways can I say that I love you?
How many ways can I show that I care?
You could walk to the ends of the earth just to leave me,
But if you should return I will always be there.

How many times can I stress my devotion?
How many times can I hold you so tight?
You could spit in my face if you chose, yet you know
That my arms still reach out for your love every night.

How many days do I sit there, just thinking?
How many nights do I lie back and cry?
Precious love, my sweet darling, please realise this
That without your sweet loving I'd die.

Mike Hall

OCEANS APART

It must be almost twenty years
Since we first met at a family *do.*
You and Patricia wore yellow
Me? Well I was in blue!

Ten years on, we met again
You flew over for a visit
No-one was sure what to expect
But I'm real glad you did it.

We've kept in touch by letter
I once called you on the 'phone.
To hear your voice was fantastic
To pay the bill, I took out a loan!

Although the ocean divides us
You have a special place in my heart
And no matter what life may bring us
We'll never be far apart.

You're a very special person
To me in every way
I'm sorry I can't be there
To share your wedding day

I know that you'll look gorgeous
As you walk along the aisle
And if you feel a bit nervous
Think back ten years and smile.

Lynne Clarke

THE DOG HOUSE

I wash the dishes and clean the floor
Vacuum around and paint the door

I clean the windows, go to the shop
Oh that reminds me I need a new mop

I make the beds, and dust around
The milkman calls, he wants ten pound

I sow some plants and mow the lawn
Darn it that's done it my dress is torn

I clean the toilet, the sink, the bath
Who's that coming up my path

I peel the spuds and make the pie
If he knew what was in it, I would die

I've done all there is even cleaned the brass
And now I'm going to sit on my . . .

But as soon as I sit the baby's awake
He's crying and moaning, his bottle I make

We build some lego for an hour of play
And go to the park to end the day

I'm tired, worn out and in a mood
In need of some rest and maybe some food

It's seven o'clock and baby's in bed
Hubby will be home soon, so he said

A quick tidy up before he comes home
For we don't want him to grumble or moan

In he comes all bubbly and bright
And says 'My goodness this house looks a sight.'

I serve him spuds and meat pie for his dinner
'It's lovely' he says adding 'for a beginner'

I smile to myself for the first time today
For it's dog's meat pie but I will not say.

S C Witts

ELUSIVE SLEEP

Where hides sleep, I can't be sure.
It's not under the pillow or on the bedroom floor.
I looked high and low after you'd fled.
I even searched under the bed.

I'm still awake at one and two.
What am I supposed to do.
I play a song, then read a book.
And after take another look.

And where hides sleep, it's still not here.
Even though morning's near.
It's not in the wardrobe or folded in a drawer.
It isn't any wonder why my eyes are so sore.

So I play a tune on my old guitar.
I sit and wonder where you are.
The guitar sounds sad and lonely too.
Just like me now we're through.

And still no sleep, it's so well hidden.
It serves me right, your love was forbidden.
Maybe tomorrow when I fall exhausted in a heap.
I'll be able to find that elusive sleep.

Dawn Stroud

ETERNITY

The mountain said to the boulder,
'When you're a little older you'll erode away.'
The boulder in reply said,
'So will you one day.'
The volcano, sneering on hearing this, said,
'I am eternal; my heart's on fire; the weather tries:
But I get higher.'
The sea heard this wicked boast,
Speaking from its foaming coast, said,
'I can extinguish you; if that's what I choose to do.
I could pour into your throat and leave behind a puff of smoke.
It is plain to see, I'm eternal, me, the sea.'
Helios, from afar - the seeing star - said,
'Sea, you must know your place:
I could devour you, leave no trace;
I could dry your puny self up:
Like a wight drink from a cup.
To be eternal, this can be only one:
You need to learn all, 'tis me the mighty sun.'
The universe said,
'Listen friends: You dwell in me; stop when I end;
And because I know I'll always be:
The mightiest must be ad infinitum . . . me.'
The boy and girl held hands,
Feeling like a grain of sand.
The immortality question beckoned;
Existence, fraction of a second.
They kissed in bliss, face to face:
Love filled every space.
Saturate the universe when the rind rolls in the hearse.

Michael Nilsen

SLEEP

Dreams of glory
Dreams of giants
With bated breath
From the precipice of Death
Knights - clad in armour
Swords flashing - and then
A scream rents the air
And you awake
Where?
A sigh of relief - safe in bed
Not dead
As you thought, as he chopped off your head
The wind howling
Scowling
Drops of rain
On the window pane
Eyes close as skies open
Sleep again
God has spoken.

Dennis R Rowe

HEED

Weed wasteful weary weak
hash, harmful, heedless hurt
speed senseless subtle suicide
cocaine careless cruel crippling
pot petty pitiful pointless
grass gangrenous gripping grief
heroin heartless hopeless hate
drugs deceptive decisive *death.*

R Stevens

RISING EAGLE

I want to write you poems
Whisper in your ear
about the wind that whistles
and everything I hear

You take my soul up high
It reaches to the sky
So please rising eagle
talk and tell me why

Although you're far away
in a barren distant land
Someday you will come back
and gently hold my hand.

Help me oh, great and
Wiser Spirit just to understand
Why my heart and soul
fly above this land.

One tiny little pebble
one sparking grain of sand
Together we are mighty
we rule the tribes of Man.

You don't know how you touched me
There are no words to say
But maybe you will come back
I will hear you say

Take my heart my darling
It's yours, now go and play.

Yvonne Dickinson

JUSTICE

Justice! For those who understand,
The riddles of the draughtsman's hand,
For those who read the judge's rhymes,
And wait for updates in the Times.
Justice for those who can confess,
To a lawyer's renowned prowess,
But where the many are concerned,
The statutes may as well be burned.

So statements found in common use,
Like 'ignorance is no excuse,'
Are just as fair on common man,
As the government's protest ban,
And just about the fairest thing,
Is that when the advocates sing,
We find that if they make mistakes,
Then ignorance is their escape.

So if you want to roll the ball,
To Parliament's almighty hall,
Make sure your pockets brim with gold,
For those to whom our rights are sold,
And if your coffers pass the test,
Be sure to give yourself a rest,
But if you lie in poverty's field,
You cannot reap the crop you yield.

Marie Newbery

A KIND OF IMMORTALITY (REMEMBERING MY FATHER)

So,
You weren't immortal after all,
at least not your body. I think it
surprised the both of us, you and
me, for you to suddenly go.

I don't suppose we needed the dramatic
farewells, because we knew we would
always end up together, in some historic
niche somewhere over cigars and beer,
or the other place's equivalent.

Our ways are different to those of others.
You and I, we carry something I could
never understand before we both grew up,
an empathy, under the intolerance, for
all those who suffer. I hope you didn't.

My mourning for you consists of work and
trying to carry all those not as bulky as I
of spirit and flesh. I suppose you learned
from me as I from you. It will never be
correct for some that we are patriarchs somehow.

So,
I miss you, but we have already
spoken in my dreams. My son has
smiled at your invisible spirit.
We shall keep meeting, I know.

Richard Pierce-Saunderson

THE FALL

Autumn's come, the air has changed
It's much, much colder outside,
The dew on the grass stays till noon
The weather has changed its tide.

Winter's near, the leaves are falling
Making a carpet of brown and red.
Conkers fall from chestnuts high
Onto a golden leafy bed.

Mice and squirrels collect their nuts
Ready for the sleep ahead,
Hibernating through the winter
With acorns and cobs to keep them fed.

I'm sitting here by the fire
The harsh North wind's blowing cold.
Soon the soft spring will come again
And new lives will be born from old.

Jemima Peacock

APARTHEID

The Power that lied.

    The Nation denied.

        The Soul that died.

            The Release that revived.

                The End of Apartheid

Steve Dunville

THE ULTIMATE CHOICE

I feel as free as a bird in flight,
gliding along on the breeze.
There'll be nothing to run from, no battles to fight,
in this pain free world of ease.

The tunnel of light that surrounds me.
stretches away to the right.
Behind me, a child is praying,
that his father will fight for his life.

I could turn my back on heaven,
and return to a life of pain.
To be there for those that need me,
I must let the suffering remain.

The tunnel of lights disappearing now,
I'm flying, like a dove,
I'm willing to crashland in reality,
and suffer for those that I love.

P Lattimore

GRANDMA

Old hag in her hospital chair,
wrinkled flesh, no life to spare.
Bad apple, shrivelled prune.
She croaks and whispers nothing new.

Who has done this to my Grandma?
My belief in God lessened by far,
If he exists why can't he . . .
No! . . . He doesn't or she . . .

No God would let a believer rot,
live a death in her baby's cot.
No world would let her disappear,
unless . . . well, it's her mind I fear.

Her body is frail, her mind's getting there,
but there's a glimmer of hope, some life somewhere.
The light that glows her face, a bit,
in the quarry of her mind is her humour pit.

T Stephens (16)

TEENAGER IN TROUBLE

Just a kid looking out of the bedroom window
For the very last time.

They never understand, they never try to.
I rebel against the emotions
They have built up inside of me.

Where does one find a sense of belonging?
Where does one find their real identity?

They make me sad.
They make me feel alone.
What has happened to the security of love.
And what become of the beautiful dreams
I have lost so many days, months, years
Searching for a dream that just wasn't there.

I can't really say I don't care
I don't think they played very fair.

With one hand resting on the suitcase
A tear falls down the side of the face.
Fear is now taking its place.
I know it's too late.
It's time for me to say goodbye
Before I just break down and cry.

Renata Kovacs

THE WEATHER

The wind is howling,
The trees are creaking,
The sunlight is blazing through the cold dismal windows,
The ground is wet and the windows
are slowly dripping dry.
The sky moves on its way
another day will have passed.
All is quiet and still
Not a movement in sight or
sound to hear,

The sun begins to rise
Slowly the moles and night creatures
move back to the underworld.

Slowly the wind begins to howl,
now but only now, another day has begun.

Helen Saunders (11)

HUMBER

I have a photograph of my father (age 22)
He is leaning, one pale arm outstretched,
hand against the wing of a black Humber
He is thin, emaciated almost,
in drainpipes and white T-shirt,
the other hand clenched,
his fist
a sign

How bold he was
he, who I once threatened with a knife
and mothers always stand by their sons
but I have your temper dad
and I am sorry for the taking
of sides.

Mark Renney

TOO LATE

I cannot believe that it has come and gone,
Now the memories are all that remain,
At the time the summer seemed so long,
Everybody prayed for rain,
It's so long since our last heatwave,
You get so used to the British weather,
What's in for these winter days?
In this cold dark November,
The smell of fireworks in the air,
Festivity brings the usual spend,
Then Easter eggs everywhere,
With the Year not even at its end.

Summer Holidays advertised on TV
As we wait for January snow,
Packing away the Christmas Tree,
Wondering where did the last year go?
Resolutions already broken,
Every year it's the same old way,
Well, you were only joking,
There is always tomorrow then it's yesterday,
Putting things off, we will never learn,
Time's the one thing that won't wait,
As we watch the seasons turn,
Tomorrow becomes too late.

Shaun Gallagher

WILL ANYONE SEE?

Swirling dust,
Carried by the wind,
Dances amongst the piles of rubble.
Blackened tree skeletons, silhouetted
Against a lifeless,
Crimson,
Glowing
Sky.
Misty haze disguises,
Once dominating buildings,
That lie crumbled on the ground.
Littering the desolate landscape
Shrivelled,
Black
Grasses
Snap in the grasp of the hot wind.
Deformed,
A battered saucepan,
Clatters along the scarred, dusty track,
Ending abruptly in the gutter,
Like the rest of the world.

Kelly Dagg

WITH NO BEGINNING - WITH NO END

My hand is a velvet silk
Smooth and soft
My face is amongst blowing velvet sheets
My eyes are in fields of cotton
My breath is amongst the highest mountains
My feet are on soft bouncy green grass with daisies and buttercups
My hair is in the wind swirling with the breeze.

Shazia Afzal

LIFE IN THE IMAGINATION

'I wear my house like a husk,
Where inside I weave
My magic spells at dusk.
Where the essence of Witch,
Hangs webbed in a mist,
Dangerously lurking,
Yet the ancient secrets
Remain faithfully held within.'

You can live a thousand light lives in the imagination,
Be a multitude of your twinkling selves,
Enjoy all the exhilarating senses,
That by instinct are yours alone,
Taking every rejuvenation that Nature offers besides.

You may safely escape into fantasy,
Away from the cold, greying world.
Beware you however,
The extremities of Guilt, infiltrating silently,
Propelling us deep into the realms of beyond,
Where a darkened force will come to rule.

Let the senses take over that reason,
Even when they say that you're mad.
For the quest must be taken towards discovery,
Reclaiming imagination as yours.

Life utterly in the Imagination,
Is it a weapon upon life itself?
Or is it just simply transcendent bliss,
A blossoming process like a kiss?
So perhaps if there be a moral to this tale,
Then it would be
To use your imagination well.

M D Dance

A FIRST AWARENESS OF TERMINAL ILLNESS
(Dedicated to a very special lady - Pamela Rhodes Owen
07-02-45 - 29-03-94)

And Suddenly . . .

Just a check up the Doctor said
Leaning over the hospital bed
Could it be the thing I dread
Nothing to worry about he said

Thorough was the word they used
Why is I feel just terribly abused
Breasts pressed against stainless steel plinths
Examination of glands they call lymphs

Legs spread apart - Christ I hope I don't fart
I'm told that this is only the start
What do they think these medical men
As they delve into places that nobody's seen

The questions they ask seem quite unrelated
Like when was the last time you were constipated
With dignity and pride so hard to retain
My thoughts are constant and I'm suffering pain

Nothing was found but still concern
An exploratory op was how they'd learn
And learn they did - A tumour was found
And all I could think of, was a hole in the ground

I thought today about my life, dependant upon a surgeon's knife
I'm told today the words I don't wish to hear, that I have been given -
just a year.

The past few months have taken their toll, now they wish to take my soul
Why me I cry as most would say, am I looking forward to today

Flowers bloom and then are spent, is it because they are heaven sent
Returned to pod by will of God, yet soon I'm destined, to lie under sod

I meditated the other day and found myself so far away
I wanted to stay and never return, but reality of life can be quite firm

Am I selfish to want to live, I feel I have so much to give
If it's God's will I still will fight, I will never acknowledge I've seen the light.

A J Havard

THE GIFT

Imagine if death meant virtue
and only the good could die

Imagine if we all knew its gift
and we aimed for the highest high

Imagine if death was a friend
which cradled us from fear

Imagine if all sinners
lived on year upon painful year

Imagine the end of bloodshed
Imagine the end of war
Imagine our fight against temptation
if lost, would extend our sentence more

Imagine if we freed our minds
and changed our daily song
removed our past anxieties
knowing that it will not be long

So next time you face the sunshine
look up and through the sky
smile softly to yourself
and whisper,
'What a beautiful day to die.'

Elizabeth Assad

AMPUTATION

Battle-weary, heartbroken,
The wounded soldier sat up in bed.
Welcomed his visitor.

'The amputations have been a complete success.
Clean, concise cuts, I'm pleased to say.
I mean, I miss each of my lovers every day
But those parts that are missing? Hell,
Reminds me how things are better this way.'

The visitor reached over, fed him grapes
Through the hole that was once his mouth.

'You defy the laws of logic.
Although parts of you have been taken away
You offer more than you did yesterday.
I'm baffled how parts of you can be missing
Yet you seem more whole than ever before?'

'Ha, I've traded the parts for wisdom, knowledge.
The cost was high but the pain was worth it.
I have come out this side a different man
For I know now what I don't want in life.'

And with that, the first genuine tear
The wounded soldier had ever shed rolled
Down from where an eye used to dwell.

Matthew Bourn

RARE SPECIES
(Dedicated to Danielle Green)

When I felt lost and lonely,
And I had nowhere to go,
You listened and understood,
And stopped me feeling low.
When I had no self-confidence,
And confusion did surround,
You gave me your helping hand,
And got my feet back on the ground.
When I felt I had nothing left,
And all I could do was cry,
You made it all just disappear,
Helped me hold my head up high.
Your smile so warm, strange it may sound,
And your eyes so true and kind,
Like a guiding light, brought me out of my shell,
The right path I did find.
You listen and understand, you make me laugh,
In myself you make me believe,
But if anything did happen, though I'm sure it will not,
Only over this friendship I would grieve,
I have known you for years, but not really well,
And I think that it is a shame,
It took so long to find such a friend,
But I won't look for someone to blame
Funny and witty, with a sense of humour,
In my heart, I know that you care,
So thank you, I shall, for being such a friend,
You're a species that is truly rare.

Anita Kalyan (16)

SEEING DOUBLE (BREASTS AND STANDARDS)

They like them up on hoardings
and on their TV screens.
On Page three of the Dailies
in top-shelf magazines . . .

They ogle them on beaches
Some *cor-ll out for a feel*
But
A few still gripe in cafés
if baby wants a meal!

Sarayen Day

ISLAND SUMMER

Fragments of early memory,
Of rock-pools, seaweed, small crabs in the sand,
Hot sun, a convent bell, steep, sanded roads
Golden in sunshine.

Clear memories of later years.
A wood with hidden waterfall;
Small, ancient farms; a meadow searched
For rare wild orchids.

Then from the air, a sunlit view
Of the whole island. And for me,
The memory of summers there,
And the depth of peace.

K Gray

SONNET TO THE VALE

Deemed flat and featureless; lowland lying
Encased three sides by rolling hills;
Partially locked, a prisoner, crying:
Your pock-marked landscape slowly fills
With spoil of man; his cultured waste,
Sinisterly sinking 'neath your clay-capped crust.
If few men want the future faced;
Fewer still are viewed with trust
By those who live within your bounds,
And see far more than Bunyan's slough.
Some dream greenery and natural sounds;
Most now drowned by motored row;
Lost to humanity's serried boxes, fields
Which once knew horse and plough.

John Kempton

HOLY SEPULCHRE OR CIRCUS?

Lady of the head-dress reassure his children from deceiving despair
Splendour remains our final wish
Pictures within his son's tombs, smirking sin
Sentence Cameras of falseness behind gates of tourism
Awake refreshed to a cockerel's ode avoiding false lenses
Church of Man *This is not a circus!*
Is there still a whispering taste of human belief?
Beggars and cripples have now the divine right to choose
Does answers lie within the holy sepulchre wall?
Christianity's birthplace
Visit God's country replenish your hidden faith
Emerge from your solemn caves
Don't be frightened
Remember it was not your hands and feet nailed upon a carpenter's creation
All martyrs wear their own crown of thorns.

Martyn Leslie Hyde

MEMORIUM

What viperous urge betook you, fool!
Such malice on your tongue.
To spite, and smite, and vilify;
Your babies,
Every one.

What grievances you threw at us,
Self martyr, yes! That's won,
Saw only imperfections in
Your babies,
Every one.

Attacking us, Oh! foolish heart,
Through all the ageing years,
We held the pain, withheld the tears
Your babies,
Every one.

And so resounding, Death's last call,
Oh! Matriarch of Many,
In solitude you died, ah me!
Your babies
Didn't come

M Kelly

LOVE

As you stood there my love for you grew, and
My life flashed by in a second.
I dared myself to tell you I love you.
But I couldn't bring myself to tell you,
Celina, if you can read this, I love you.
I know you think I must be shy, beyond my
Love for you.
But underneath I am a free spirit destined to
Be with yours

Laura Benbow (9)

90

A SUMMER'S DREAM

Now Winter time has finally past,
And summer time is here at last,
The birds and bees come out to sing,
For what the new months have to bring,
The woodland creatures had just awoke,
To find that Winter time had broke,
As the sun shines high up in this sky,
The young birds spread their wings to fly.

The flowers had now come to bloom,
For it was that summer day of June,
The harvest time was coming near,
And all young lambs were soon to shear,
The trees had now begun to leaf,
As young kids climbed that rocky reef,
The breeze was now so nice and cool,
As the frogs sat in that muddy pool.

Had summer time come to a finish at last,
The mist grew thick and strong so fast,
The dew fell on the grass so sweet,
The woodland creatures knew it was time to sleep,
The birds now tucked up in their nest,
Knew finally it was time to rest.

The snow falls hard at winter time,
The trees left bare they have no mind,
As animals now lay down to rest,
And dream of summer at its best,
And when they wake of Spring time fear,
And hope for yet another sunny year,
So all the animals that you hear,
Are the ones that sleep right through the year.

James Folan

FINAL NOTES OF A BOY
(ON EXPEDITION TO THE CAIRNGORMS)

There is no shelter:
Only the barren outcrops of ice-tipped rock
And jagged sheets of purple stone
Jutting like prehistoric blades
Through the frozen soles of our boots.
The snow-capped wind splinters our bones.
When the vast climb gets steep,
It presses our numb raw cheeks
Against the vertical. Exhausted,
We cannot sleep for shivering
While the wind jabs ceaselessly
Our Polaris.

There is no shelter.
Not anywhere.
None of us imagined this.
Not at the border.
Not at base camp.

Mac is relentless.
He says we must push on.
No rest.
Not now.
He thinks we'll make it,
Time, I think,
Is running out.

Catherine Rose

FLOWERS FOR GRANDMAMA

Flowers are so beautiful,
They heraldeth the spring,
I gather in my apron
Held up with coloured strings.

The road is long an upward hill,
I gather whilst I play,
The guarded flowers of hedgerows,
And the white sweet scented *May*

The buttercups and daisies,
Anemones oh so sweet,
Cowslips and bluebells
What a wondrous treat.

To take them home to Grandmama,
Brings back her youthful days.
Of meadows filled with king-cups,
And her body wrapped in *stays.*

Of flouncing skirts and petticoats,
And running in the sun.
But now her youth is over,
Her lifespan nearly done.

Arranging all these meadow flowers,
In vase bought long ago.
Brings happiness to Grandmama,
And tears begin to flow.

But though this life is ending,
My grandmama doth know.
That flowers abound in *heaven above.*
Just as here on *Earth below.*

Clare Bright

MY SON

The day you were born was a wonderful day,
The way that I felt I could never say,
The gift of a son, so healthy and strong,
Such a wonderful joy after waiting so long.

The love that you gave me I will always treasure,
And watching you grow gave me endless pleasure,
You became my close friend and my confident too,
And I love being with you just because you were you.

As time passed by and you changed to a man,
To help and to guide you I still do what I can,
Now things have changed and we're living apart,
But never forget that you're still in my heart.

Not one day goes by that I don't think of you,
I would like to think that you feel that way too.
If you concentrate hard you will feel my embrace
And the gentle pressure of my kiss on your face.

Whenever you're worried or just feeling blue,
Remember your mum is still thinking of you,
My arms are around you, I'm holding you tight,
I'm giving you my love with all of my might.

Wherever you are and whatever you do,
I want you to know that I'll always love you,
Whatever the distance whatever the time,
Whatever your age you will always be mine.

Jean Adams

THE COTTAGE

All that I own before me lies
As dawn's light through the shutters steals
Swords of gold cutting the gloom.
Dust, disturbed by shallow slumber,
drifts upon the morning rays.
Points of light, like stars upon the wall,
creep down toward my resting place.
The ruffled blankets scarce raised upon,
this frail and fading body
An indentation on the mattress,
such as a ghost would leave,
pressed upon the summered heads of weary corn,
which now awaits the reaper's scythe.
As I now wait.
Dappled drops of sunlight rest heavy on
a gnarled and weathered face,
sallow skin, drawn taut in earlier times,
now hangs in the hollows 'twixt cheek and jowl.
Deep caverns, dark rimmed, watery,
where once a sparkling blue.
The shutters fly open and rattle,
like wind in an old man's chest.
Light flooding in, destroys my sanctity.
Through the tear stained windows, a field.
Our field of hopes and dreams that would feed
us in our Autumn years.
It broke our hearts and spirits endlessly.
The lush green rows of corn now rise to mock
me. Hah!
And now too late, the planting all done,
save one clear place 'neath a willow tree
and that's where they'll be planting me.

William J Surman

AFTERNOONS THE BOMBERS HEADED BACK

Going over a Belgrade suburb
halfway home and the bombs not shed
he sloughed them on the open city;
I am the hero and you are dead.

This lady trudged to the cemetery
for many years after the war.
She'd got home, and her house was standing,
but the children had gone next door.

Later, my uncle visited England
and brought me back a splendid doll,
but made me say it came from Paris;
so many empty desks at school.

That's why my Yugoslav acquaintance
looks cock-eyed at a British plane.
But fifty years have passed like cloud cones
and now the bombers fly again.

Merryn Williams

MY FIRST LOVE

Tonight I cannot sleep at all
For in the morning you will call
To hear your voice, to see you smile
Will make the waiting all worthwhile
I don't know why I feel this way
It's puppy love my friends will say.
But we both know that they are wrong
Puppy love is not this strong.
This love is something I'll never regret
For you are my first love I'll never forget.

Tracy Fountain

DISCRIMINATION

It doesn't matter what colour you are, whether you're black or white,
You shouldn't be discriminated against for any reason, it just isn't right.
It shouldn't make a difference if you're clever, strong or weak,
It shouldn't make a difference how we look or how we speak.
It shouldn't matter what clothes we wear, or if we limp when we walk,
And does it really matter if we stutter or stammer when we talk?
We shouldn't be laughed at because of our age or our name,
We are all different, wouldn't it be boring if we were all the same?
Because of our beliefs we shouldn't be rejected,
We all have different points of view and these should be respected.
We've seen what discrimination has done in the past, we have seen the
results,
So we should respect everyone around us . . . because we all have our faults.

Dawn Rumsey

LEAVING TITHONUS

Amid the hypnopompic haze,
Dawn ascends the sublime skyway.
Fusing the ink-black, jet-black empyrean,
With the ascending aurora of glimmering phosphorescence,
Luring the night into impassioned impotence.
Completing another cycle in the perpetual gauntlet for the meridian.
Slowly the tingling sheen evolves,
Tinging the clear sky with pigments of sensibility.
Gradually the blushing complexion of the sky transmutes
Into a blazing, contorted, vision of wild fire.
Reacting with the rising spirit to create an ephemeral air of
awe and serenity.

Claire Every

I DO NOT KNOW

As I lie here, ghosts of my past float around my head
I can't remember the night before, or was it tomorrow
I do not know.
Oblivion beckons me closer, giving me promises of
Sanctuary within its walls, why does it call me.
I do not know.
My life is difficult to remember, mists cloud my thinking
Problems I have had fade into nothing, is this good.
I do not know.
Oblivion calls me with increasing urgency it is
Difficult to resist, life is fine with Oblivion, or is it.
I do not know.
Why do I find that my life looks better through a haze
How can I live when I do not know what living is.
I do not know.
Are there others that think this way, how do they cope
Maybe Oblivion copes for them as it does for me.
I do not know.
Is Oblivion dangerous, are all it's promises lies
I don't think they are, am I wrong to trust it.
I do not know.
When the time comes for Oblivion to take me forever
Will it look after me then as it does now.
I do not know.
Or will the mists clear and will I be left alone in the
Darkness fully aware of what my life has been like.
I do not know.
What is it like to be aware of life, complete with all its
problems and Hardships, but being able to overcome them.
I wish I knew.

R Haynes

VOICES IN MY HEAD

The whisper through the cobwebs,
Of the times I left behind.
Of forgotten friends and promises,
Of the days when I was blind.

They sing to me of better days,
A melancholy song
Was it such a glorious time?
Could I have been so wrong?

My thoughts play tricks,
They twist and turn.
No respite can I find
My body yearns to switch to sleep
But I can't switch off my mind.

Who are these strangers in my head?
Who let them slip inside?
I can't escape! they seek me out!
There is no place to hide.

I wonder, when will I be free
To make my life my own?
Will they aspire to live in peace?
In the mind they've made their home.

Or can I kill whom they may be
Their infernal chatter dead?
Or will they always stay with me?
The voices in my head.

Through buried memories twix and twine,
I stalk them silently.
I cannot stay the stranger's noise,
For the *stranger* here is me..

Theresa Gallagher

THE MARY ROSE

Off she went to fight in the war
Waved to by Henry on the shore.
This was his flag ship, the pride of the fleet,
Sailing to glory the French to meet.

That Tudor warship packed with men
Never to see their homes again.
Too many marines, too many guns
Makes her float deep as before tide she runs.

Her gun ports are open showing her power,
This beautiful ship, this Tudor flower.
Her men have all eaten fish, peas and mead.
Of drink they've had plenty - perhaps more than they need.

They are gathering about in uneven group
Which unbalances this overloaded sloop.
A sudden wind! A gusty squall!
Sea rushes in gun ports - down she must fall!

Over seven hundred men went down to the deep,
To that watery grave of endless sleep.
The pride of the nation was no more.
He'd nothing to wave to the king on the shore.

It is hundreds of years since she went
Lying there buried in the silt of Solent.
But once more she is up from the foam,
Restored and admired in her museum home.

Val Trantum

MEMORIES

In our old town, before the war,
We had a yearly treat,
It was the local carnival,
Where all the folks would meet.

There was a long procession,
Which wandered round the town,
Floats were *dressed up to the nines*
Plus many a budding clown.

Grove gardens were the venue
For that day of happy fun,
The stalls sold out, the band played on,
Until the day was done.

Alas, the clouds of war came down,
The carnivals were ended,
Grove house became the offices
On which this town depended.

The lovely building played its part,
I worked a while there too,
The room which was my office then
Is now the disabled loo.

The carnivals have now come back,
Let's hope they bring a touch
Of the healthy fun we had before,
Which we enjoyed so much.

Isobel Crumley

ONCE

Once I could hear the waves beat on the shore,
See the sunset blush the sky.
Walk for miles at least a score,
Passing all others by.

Once I could crack a nut between my teeth,
Bite an apple to the core.
At night lie upon my back to sleep,
While never known to snore.

Once I could run to catch the last train,
Never miss a trip.
Though crazy once jumped from a plane,
Thought my mind would flip.

Once I could paint the house both in and out,
Climbing the ladder high.
By lunch hoovered, dusted turned rooms about,
With washing out to dry.

Now as I sit here day by day,
Life has lost all lustre.
To get myself on knees to pray,
All energy must muster.

No more can hear the waves beat on the shore,
Or see the sky turn red.
All that's left in life to hope for,
To die peacefully in my bed.

Pamela Stone

WORDS OF WARNING

I do not know what he has told you
but if he can lie to me -
his love for 12 years
the person he proposed to
his soul-mate
his intimate play-mate
the mother of his unborn child -
then he can sure as hell lie to you
who are nothing
but a party to his deceit

He says you are just a *symptom*
(that's flattering)
that you are unimportant
that it could have been anyone
He says that sex with you -
notice he does not say love-making
because he does not love you -
is unremarkable
He says he hates cats -
but especially yours

You would be wise to leave well alone
unless you wish to suffer
for I will not let him go -
I love him
and he loves me - he tells me all the time

You are just a minor temporary distraction
his little guilty secret
(no longer)
and you will not be able to stay the course
once you realise the truth

Sara Cloherty

BELONGING TO

Your life is not your own,
Your mind and heart are not your own.

Life is always because of others.
Your mind is full of what others have said.
Your heart feels love or hate for others.

Living is for others' satisfaction
Loving is for others' benefit
Thinking is thoughts of others.

Dying is death of you and you alone.
When you live, you live for others
When you die you die alone.

A J Haughton

CRACKING THE WHIP

To have faith in this world is a difficult task,
Who's telling the truth, who's wearing a mask.

To believe what you read, and absorb what you see,
Might be a mistake, it's only TV.

Constantly shocked about everyday news,
Corrupt politicians creating hardship and blues.

Police propaganda a now every day thing,
Their claims seem to have a familiar ring.

Hammer the motorist because of concern,
Or an easy touch target for the cash they have earned.

I long for the day when all becomes clear,
To be rid of this farce and society's tears.

Things can be better, I know that they can,
But changes are made by all, not by one man.

Gus Carn

HIGH ENGLAND

There is nothing more worth doing than to walk on High England,
To tread, tingling, the sheep-scythed turf
And climb the bellying moor,
Then zenith reaching,
To fling one's arms wide and feel the antiseptic wind
Refresh the body and cool the mind,
Then, silently, to stand and gaze and deeply breathe
And gasp at the glory of High England.

And then to drop down the sky again, at dusk,
To find in some hill wrapped vale,
An inn, where honest ham and eggs and apple-tart
Feed the senses and tug the heart.
Then with mine host to sit and drink the amber ale,
And hear the news from down the dale,
Of how the sheep fared at the sale
And all about November's gale.
To sit and see the horizontal sun
Glint on coloured bottles
And watch the shadow of a pipe bewitched into a giant's bowl.

John G Wilson

WAITING

I have this idea about a poem

it could be about waiting
like waiting for the phone to ring
like I'm doing now

waiting for my beloved to come home.

I found myself waiting
I find myself waiting

for repair men, the post, rain to stop, the bus,
traffic to move, in the queue at the checkout . . .

waiting to become fat
waiting to grow old

this poem could be about . . . anger . . .
. . . anger at myself for waiting forever . . .
wait . . . wait . . . wait

. . . anger at my cervix waiting . . .
waiting at the hospital in the waiting room
in the waiting room outside the examination room
waiting for the doctor . . .
waiting for what he might say
waiting for the result . . . waiting
for the result of my smear test

I am angry, angry with my cervix
how could I get this thing
I am waiting for it to be gone

my life of waiting

waiting for death

waiting for my friend to remember me . . .

waiting

Cally Barker

106

CHARON

My windy howl crescendos and bellows out
At blazing light that hurts my eyes,
Posters and people are slashed down the middle,
As I pass on
To sit and rest in the dark.
Silence almost succeeds the echoes,
Dimness numbs my thoughts,
I meditate in stasis
Awaiting rumbling doors.
I notice no people.
People do not notice me.
Only the controls and Monty's *right!*
Inform me that I exist.
I preen my secret importance,
Sometimes I strike.

It makes no difference to me
However long I wait.
The dark tunnel and echoes,
Wind and noise shaking up dust
Are my cocoon.
My eye follows the polished rails
Leading round the gaunt bend
To the bustle of Clapham North
Through which I shall also pass
To sit and rest in the dark.

Only, my back aches.
Still, I am the core of the whirlwind,
I ride the sparks and fumes,
I bear many in my deferential carriages.

Ali Cohen

FROM BEGINNING TO END

A soft white feather
A song from the sun
A violet river
A life begun
A fathomless sea
A whispering dove
A helpless sinner
A treasure of love
An empty grave
An open lock
A puzzled detective
A timeless clock
A burning sword
A lonely soul
A sinking ship
A silver scroll
A weeping spirit
A dying cloud
A falling sky
A velvet shroud
A creeping child
A laughing breath
A concluded life
A sound of death

Karen Valentine

SILENT WINDMILL

In the fading light of dusk,
Stands the ragged mill,
But now, the wind shall blow no more,
Its sails are deathly still.

No stones shall grind the heads,
Of the newly ripened corn,
No flour, to bake our bread,
For the coming morn.

Thus a hunger burns our bellies,
We'll no more have our fill,
Our end lies with the wind,
And the silent, old windmill.

I Hadden

MEN AND WOMEN

Softness is a gentle thing
A woman's touch -
A breath of Spring.
One finds it in sweet babies too
When they look at you with eyes so blue.
But harshness is a man's abode
Who fights with fire and heavy load.
Who thinks he is the King of all,
But soon finds out when he is old,
All people aren't what they seem
I know which I'd rather be
A softie woman just like me
There is too little love in life
Men are the ones who cause the strife.
But a woman with a gentle touch
Just to a man could mean so much
He'd change his life and happier be
If he could love someone like me
I know which one I'd rather be
If only *he* would come to me.

W Z Laura Moore

WE THANK YOU LORD

Dear Lord,
    We thank You,
for the sunshine that ripens the corn,
    We thank You
For the rains that comes in the morn.

How refreshing the rain
after a hot dusty day,
when men finish working
and children finish play.

But most of all, we thank You
For your Son,
For dying for us, Your will was done,
How great is Your love for each one of us
That Jesus did die upon the cross.

And thank You too
That He rose again
For death couldn't hold Him
He's broken the chains.

Dear Lord,
    Thank you for
breaking the chains that bind,
setting my whole being free,
My spirit, soul and mind.

May my love for You grow stronger
As I walk with You each day,
Trusting You always
Letting You lead the way.

Gloria Goyns

TOUCHING

Touching you
I feel the world retreat
The crowd melts down
The room is empty
Save us two.

Touching me
I know your boundaries are sound
Intact for all the world to see -
What about me?

Your words have burned my fences down
Let's be real together
Let me hold you
There's more to touch
Than flesh on flesh
Your touch has left its imprint
On my soul.
At your hands
I am exposed, then violated
So crucify me then,
But make it quick.

Let me touch you one more time
Who cares about the cost?
I've paid it
All in tears
Let me hold you
Just once more.

Rosemary Drewett

HAROLD

Eulogies are made but Red Flags not lowered
For these days the Red Roses blow on us.
Political art now shines attracting new masses
But you understood humanity comes first.

Socialism is for all seasons or reasons
Ideology must prove its feasibility.
Uniting all collars, avoiding class struggle
Till the people receive government that's fair.

You sought OU type opportunity, and fair education.
Security through redundancy's claim against failure.
Fiscal courage, knowing that the weeks are long
And justice needs an electable party to survive.

Slim Jim fell, assailed by winter's discontent
The boot came on the foot of ideology and failed
Welsh wizardry effected much but not election
And sadly John fell before he proved himself.

An new time dawns and revision is the call
This may be so and we have the man of change
If he succeeds, shall we see a social hero
While you sleep in the Isles of Saints.

Bill Cowley

FAMILY FIGHT

Mother's milk
Underscore lightly
Take the heat
Hate me or fight me

And so
Peace or
Hate

Upside of the downside
Copper moon will pull the tide
Can you see the flip side
A downside of the ringside.

Arthur J Wyatt

BLETCHLEY TO BEDFORD

Claiming the train
With gasps and gossip
The three girls with the magazine are worldy wise.
Pointing at the portraits of pin-thin mannequins
They identify where the pictures have been enhanced.
They see through the dance -
This glossy world they know to be untrue.

The pretty one, the witty one, the one who has dreams!
It seems they can picture themselves with confidence.
They dust their halos,
Brush their hair and compare notes on parental Hagiography.

Like the rest of the train
Catching winks before work,
I don't recognise myself in their conversation.
I read the same sentence in an old *Beds on Sunday*
Hoping that at some point it will make sense to me.
My critical judgement failing me.

Nodding appearing wise
I then fall asleep.

G A Stewart

AT THE MAIDEN INN

It was early in the morning,
I was feeling rather queer,
I had the strangest feeling
That somebody was near!

The half light gave a rosy glow.
My sleepy eyes could see,
A ghostly figure coming, coming,
Coming near to me.

I felt so very frightened!
This vision to see,
And then a voice, spoke out to say,
Dost thou want thy cup of tea?

I could see her now quite clearly,
Then with a ghostly pall,
She reached her hand out to me
Then vanished through the wall.

E Williams

RED RIBBON UNFURLS . . .

Tied my leather ballet shoes
Criss crossed up round my legs
When I, a young girl, danced joyously.

Belted my dress, in which I
Seduced my first lover
Into sex safe from birth and disease.

Adorned fresh white lilac
Given to celebrate
The May morn birth of my baby son.

Loops on my daughter's lapel
Stark symbol of distress.
This red ribbon binds us to world's woe.

Janet Carter

A BRIDGE CROSSED

No frittering wastrel from that echelon above, sequested
carried, and never thought of love, no-one is, no-one can,
be so macho to spurn natural life in one life's span.

Love has been, love is so, and love will emanate wherever we go
those damned eternal, love hate, gregarious themes,
Of course a man deserves a wife, but did you, could you
tear that thought and shout, 'Piffle, Bosh' that man there dreams.

I'm telling you from soul to heart, no book can, no book will
love's rules did not that impart, what looks will do why looks imbue
were not so imbecilic in their all time view.

We men like to think that we are it, never heard of their
snarling rhetoric, atones for nothing we them inconsistent pips or
future mayhem, oh could you but stand for one mellow thought
consuming hour, think back, why did you abuse her you are a fellow.

Melodramatic bleatings rent the air, oh yes I love, but why
should I care, the plague and play of all time sots, *Me marry?*
Cut me up and bury me in pots.

David Price

A CHEAT CALLED DESTINY

Love is like a drug money is that too
When you have enough you feel high
But if they say goodbye to you
You feel you want to die

> Love or money, Money or love
> It's all the same to me
> Life is just a game we play
> With a cheat called destiny

Could we live our lives once more
Would we really want to anyway
To make the same mistakes as before
It would be fated to be that way

> Love or money, Money or love
> It's all the same to me
> Life is just a game we play
> With a cheat called destiny

The dice are thrown, our future's cast
Some would say we're lucky to be alive
But the future will mirror the past
As we struggle to survive

> Love or money, Money or love
> It's all the same to me
> Life is just a game we play
> With a cheat called destiny

April Thorne

GLOVES

Where are the hands that keep us warm?
They've not been seen for some time.
They filled us with love and a sense of belonging,
But now we've been left behind.

Where are the hands that keep us warm?
Why are they not to be seen?
Thrown on a table and left to grow old,
Is this the end of our dream?

Where are the hands that keep us warm?
Where are the wrists to be covered?
Where are the fingers and thumbs that fit snug?
When will our loss be discovered?

Where are the hands that keep us warm?
We hope that they are safe and well.
We know that we'll all meet again one day,
'Hello,' we expect you to yell.

Where are the hands that keep us warm?
Why have we been left to die?
Do you not care what happens to us,
That we're sad and have started to cry?

Where are the hands that keep us warm?
Let's re-unite one day.
Please make it soon, not never at all,
But what if we've been thrown away?

David Thomas Walter

EASTER SUNDAY '93

The Easter Chick.
I've been pecking quite a time now,
To get out of this shell.
At last I think it's cracking.

This is oh so tiring,
But think I'm doing well,
At last I'm out,
I'm looking around in wonder!
This the world in which I'm
        Going to wander.

My feathers are quite wet and so,
I'll need to wait before I go
To join my sisters and brothers,
So as to get protection
        From our mother

E R Baines

MASTURBATION

Behind the glass face
of my grandmother's grandfather clock
the big hand has fallen
(like a climber from a cliff face)
and has formed a curved bridge from 5 to 7.

By the little hand
I only know the hour is 4,
but when it reaches 5
I shall play backgammon from 5 to 7.

By myself.

And cheat.

Andrew Pye

HOLIDAY HOTEL

Anyone can enter
revolve to the centre
of this covetous attention.
Mention a speciality
and it will appear -
diverse habits understood
with a suave conviviality.
The dining room expels
smells of food in variety
served by waiter/waitress
penguin-dressed as they tiptoe
and tip-finger loaded trays.
The lounge propels
the elderly to rest
in straight-backed chairs
blind to illicit affairs,
or the eager impatience
of bride and groom
in an upstairs room.
Morning brings a fresh awakening -
the ritual of hotel habits -
breakfast, English or Continental.
Guests nod morning greetings.
Bride and groom still sleeping?
And at this sober time of day
noise is a long low hush
before a coming rush.
Reception waits, groomed for more
guests to come, guests to go -
revolving with the door.

Gwynneth Curtis

SOAR

Out of the corner of my bloodshot eye
I see a young bird attempting to fly
And from the memory of my shattered mind
I remember the young bird being left behind
My right hand twitches
When I think of the switches
And the buttons that support me now
I feel like the bird trying to fly
But only falling to the ground.

I feel like a baby being born to this land
A terrifying experience by a menacing hand
Surrounded by unfamiliar faces
Looking like a lost sheep in various phases
Born again it's black into blue
'There's nothing more we can do.'

The bird lays bleeding, it's broken its wing
The feathers are ruffled and it can't sing
We failed our first life
We never got to roar
But in the world above
We will both soar.

Sean Brown

PRISONER WITHIN

Prisoner within your walls of dreams and passions and failures too,
You are among an endless scorn of wrongs and rights you feel,
Uniforms pass your way, table manners and duties of another day,
You stand alone of painful mind and if you let it can go blind.
Of all you stood for just time before, don't let go.

So many different walks of life combined to live you must,
All favours are so little and friends are only just,
Cell mates don't know too much and some they know you all,
Prisoner within your walls, don't let yourself fall.

Heather Creighton

OLD FAITHFUL

I have a car I call my steed
Without it I'd be lost.
I call it my old banger
Bought at little cost.

It is a little rusty
So I treat it with great care
But it is so reliable
It takes me everywhere

The inside looks quite tatty
The seats are bare and torn
It purrs along quite happily
And has a noisy horn

What would I do without it
To me it's like a toy
It may be old and rusty
But it's something I enjoy

If some day, it will not start,
With my old banger I'll not part.
I have a good mechanic friend
My old banger he can mend
To purr along quite happily
And go everywhere with me.

Bob Reynolds

BULLY

School is over, kids rush out
heading homeward end of day
'cept the few who furtive creeping
keeping out of bullies' way
Said he'd wait when school was over
Said he'd fix us good this time
Unless handing over fifty pence
Pays for protection that's no crime
Up and down the road they scanned
From the safety of the gate
Too many places for him to hide in
Too many alleyways to wait
Let's take a chance and stick together
We can make it to the bus
There's no-one here so let's get going
We'll make it quicker if we rush
Across the road and round the corner
down the alley breathing fast
Racing fast as legs will take them
No-one wanting to be last
At end of alley a dark shadow
detaching from a darker mass
steps in front to block their flight
Arms outstretched so none can pass
Without pounding hearts from fright and running
the trio halt their hopeless race
look up with dread for their tormentor
But instead find a friendly face
The PC watches as they amble
around the corner to their bus
Thinking that kids never change
Always have to be in a rush

Across the road a boy stands watching
Unnoticed by the trio now
Decides to see them all tomorrow
One at a time, they'll pay, somehow.

J W Wallace

THE SEA

I dread to think
how it might be
If the mighty sea
encompassed me.
I cannot swim,
I cannot float,
The sea is large
And that's no joke.
If I should paddle
too far out
The sea would wash me
all about.
And if I sank
beneath the sea,
The fish would not
be pleased with me.
Upon the pier
perhaps I'll stand
And watch the sea
embrace the land.

June Rampton

20TH CENTURY FOOL

The night is bitter,
The cold air bites,
I'm basking in warmth,
and snuggled up tight.

As far as I see,
nothing matters - but *me*
I could spare you a minute,
though, of course - at a fee.

'I think I'm dying, the ill man stuttered,
Please can you take me away from the gutter.'
'I've a life of my own,' the rich man replied.
And with a toss of his head - he just walked on by.

You shouldn't ignore it -
or even deplore it
I know that you're lying when you tell me
you're blind.

Hypocrisy's breeding,
Manifesting and feeding.
Please treat his wounds,
when he's battered and bleeding.

Lisa Merryweather

TREMBLING

Lying there, under the heap of rubble
The motions of the earth tremble
Quietly at first the drill moves in and out
Edging its way in
Penetrating further with every movement

Devouring it as it goes
The earth rumbles louder in an almost pre-historic manner
It's almost, as if it knows what's coming
It's been used and moulded before
It's nothing new
Same action different tools

It shakes violently under the pneumatic drill
It watches itself move in time
It cannot stop
The cogs turn the wheel of life!

Sarah Wilde

AT DAWN

With dawn the sky was grey
for through the night dew had drenched old earth
A waking sun tried hard to pierce the ridge
Between the empty space so far away
her golden drapes did bridge
Will day be fair and warm.
And rays of sun collect the tears of night
Or like a naughty child let shadows dark
And great black clouds run wild
to hide away the light
Crushing out every breath of warmth and cheer
Leaving earth so cold and drear
Keep back the wind and rain
and wild clouds flying
Wait until the day has gone
And the sun is dying.

Christina Young

NOTHING IS IMPOSSIBLE

All the meat lies frozen
The fishcutter calls your name
On these basest nights
You are free
This, they cannot prevent
Unwelded goodbyes
There is no shame in denying
Words have limitations
As do womankind
Everything is permitted
And when I begin
Come not briefly for him
It's not veal you're eating
You may laugh
Everything is permitted
The overnight ice-breaker
The laughter of small animals
Your dead father - insignificant
Overnight freight is less expensive
On these basest nights
There is no shadow in denying.

Paul Rafferty

THE KIDS OF KIDLINGTON

The kids of Kidlington
are raucous and scrawny
as fledglings,
they wheel on their bikes
at odd angles,
curse and chew gum
like film stars.

They kick footballs and each other
in a school of hard knocks,
getting roughly scuffed
into shape
for a slambang of factory.
Their eyes
are full of childhood.

Alistair Ricketts

DEAD

If I start to feel my own small blunt pain.
The shame that I must face, I must face alone.
To face alone, to face that evolving poor shame.
The penetrations that kill, the hole is theirs to fill.
Dying, once trying, I can hardly strain to hear.
To hear is to diminish, diminish is to siphon life.

Plunder, my life is not too idyllic in my own ways.
The simple things are no longer easy to do.
Simple things are ideal in humorous situations.
The body shrivelled so totally out of character.
My lovelight is changing into a mere chameleon.
The will jolts from me, the hunger is no longer me.

They will stand to celebrate my insufficient life.
Insufficient everyone will say, he didn't believe.
He lied the valiant will cry, I was a pawn in many.
To die in poverty, to be the bottom of the bunch.
When my dust glimmers in my light, will you think.
In years to come, who's here, just my lost soul.

David John Baxter

FORGOTTEN POWER

Stale stench stays,
As it has done for years
The lost meaning easily betrays
And with it brings many fears.

A disappearing smart flow.
Where now for those of loneliness?
Legions buried like the ground in snow.
Tragedy looms for the unconfessed.

Few overcoats buff the cracking comfort
Few gaze at the presentable riches,
Nothing is spoken, little is taught,
Neglect and sadness is all that is brought.

The door swings freely on ancient hinges,
The figure in black can only mourn.
Grass surrounding stone flickers and flinches,
The majestic houses stands only for dawn.

So silent is the past: so still the yard.
Wheels float by now and then
Through iron gates so dreadfully marred,
To avoid a scene with hand on pen.

Echoes of drops on the broken rafters
Are all that occupy and remain.
History will now never strain
To recall the intensity of present pains.

James Cook

BEACH LIFE

Litter, shingle, laughter,
children play on trampolines.
Squealing, shouting, running
to the water and back again,
sand between their toes.
Merry music in the air
A fair ground is down there.
Picnickers, sunbathers,
deck chair addicts too are
unaware of that solitaire

standing at the water's edge;
on the ribbed, red sand with
lisping waves to wash the feet.
A motor drone, the Jet Ski bounces,
windsurfers balance on the wake.
Dinghies drift their sails dazzle,
grey bellied clouds hang low,
a blanket for the pregnant sea.

The green swell arcs to welcome me.
A marionette in its lap
I greet its surge and fall;
revel in prevalent danger.
Hands on seabed, body out flat.
I turn and roll and laugh with glee
for the first time I swam in the sea.

Mary Percival

BOOT CAMP

From tower block
To courtroom dock
A young life of crime
Has got you doing time
No *easy life* electronic clamp
You're sent to a *Boot Camp*
With other offenders going barmy
It's just like the army
Where winter, spring, summer or fall
You get your early wake up call
Even if it's raining
They get you outside circuit training
Making you tone up your body
Just like some poor *squaddie*
Sure enough people will mock
The theory behind the short, sharp shock
But is it a sin
To instil self discipline
As the government believes
It'll deter young thieves
But their main worry
Is they don't come back in a hurry
So will it put an end
To the re-offend

Flakie

THOUGHTS OF AN ORPHAN LAMB

My legs are cold and hurting as I tumble to the ground
My heart is beating strongly, so I know I will be found.
I know my mum is dead now, I heard the shepherd say
We'll give her to another so she'll live another day.

I think she really likes me, she suckles me and stays
Although she has another she very rarely strays.

I'm all grown up and healthy, with others I will play
In meadows and in grasses, until the day the man comes
To take us all away.

Elizabeth A Robbins

CHRISTMAS IS COMING

Yes, it's getting nearer - the Christmas lights go on
The gifts wrapped permanently on display
The tinsel and the glitter
Of the ornaments and baubles.
Meant to tempt and tease
The money out of our pockets.
Only six weeks to go
Time to book the dinner
Half the population is worried and thinner!
So is the bank balance
What the heck it's Christmas!
Santa's, let me count them
one two three and four.
One in every store.
Merry Christmas!
The tins of the charities rattle in your face
The homeless in the doorway
All part of the human race
Wanting a share of the Christmas jingle.
Whatever happened to the peace hope and joy
Brought to us by Mary's boy?

Anni Austin

HARVESTER

At first I spotted a cloud of dust
The dust appeared the colour of rust;
When all of a sudden -
A monstrous thing appeared in the distance;
And showed its head
A monstrous thing; yellow and red!
'Twas too far away to hear any sound
Just clouds of dust billowed around;
Clouds of dust that billowed and spread -
So much at times; the fiend lost its head,
But when a breeze that there did blow
Had cleared the dust that had earlier shown
The monster's head once again appeared
But the red and yellow was now quite clear;
It was only a combine harvester!

Geoff Dennis

AUTUMN

Foggy morning bathed with dew
Autumn sunlight straining through
Springtime leaves have near diminished
Their lifespan has all but finished
Autumn colours at their best
Each one contrasts with the rest
Rustic browns the tarnished golds
Bright red berries hedgerows embellish
Thoughts of winter far from cherished

Barry Bryant

IMAGE

Every morning is hard to face,
I do not want to confront the truth,
But that is all you give to me,
For once why not tell a lie.

Every morning I have watched life drain,
From once a floating bubble of air
Willing to drift anywhere,
But instead found a grey sky.

Every morning you show me where happiness was
And where sadness and pain are,
The lines of frustration are there
And the tears I cannot cry.

Every morning you show me disease,
And how love and kindness once reigned,
Hate and bitterness dominated my world now
And yet I do now know why.

My mouth has twisted through the years,
The grey has streaked my curls,
I have dark eyes hiding dark secrets
Which I shall take with me when I die.

It is time to face the real world,
No false lashes or smiles,
I must age with dignity
And hold my head up high.

You have been harsh in your approach
For which I do not like,
Mirror, will you not even try
For once, why not tell a lie.

D J Horne

THE MIRROR

My make-up strewn across the sink
The mirror light is on
I gaze at my reflection, think
Of all the things I see as wrong.

My eyes too small, my lips too thin
My nose is out of shape.
I take my pencil and begin
To outline my escape.

Foundation serves to fill the cracks,
Then powder dulls the shine;
All plastered on like sealing wax,
My image soon will be divine.

Some blusher gives a healthy glow
To white anaemic face.
Eyeshadow and my eyes now grow
And lines are gone without a trace.

I take my lipstick and with care
Produce a sultry pout.
No longer I return my stare
Another face is looking out.

But this face is the one I seek
The one I show to him;
To compliment my toned physique
From hours in the gym.

But in the morning what remains
After our night of passion?
He'll see my spots and broken veins
And I'll have had my ration.

Jo Gray

134

INSOMNIAC

The week curves as a long-bow at his shoulder held;
One arrow there, one point of focus.
And I, between the target and the shaft
Turn to its shape,
Restless, tangling the disputed sheets;
Or lie, five senses swirled across my eyelids
Like colours on a palette.
Still as the old, or very young, know how to lie
To make anticipation satisfy.
In this dumb pause
Time's curvature plays over me by heartbeats
Making a week eternity -
Until one midnight, knowing that I wait
Launches the arrow from the tightened string
To plunge at length again into my flesh, and quiver,
And be still.

Diana Cockrill

BLUE LADY

Her paper face blinked in recognition.
A thin crooked hand sailed up,
But when I reached out it ghosted back
To its spidery companion in her lap.

Two uninvolved eyes rolled to one side.
She's going away swathed in coats,
Curling down, gentle as the air;
Sailing miles back into a big blue chair.

John Thynne

LUTON (MY HOME TOWN)

Luton is my home town
I'm a thoroughbred through and through.
My parents, and their parent's parents
All were born here too.
The town that I remember was much quieter by far,
Where people used to walk, instead of getting out the car.
Each Sunday we would walk with our children, hand in hand,
All the way to Wardown Park, and listen to the band.
We'd play some golf, then feed the ducks,
The Museum we would see,
The children always gazed in awe at our local history.
We had dances on the moor, and oh! We had such fun.
Always it would seem that we knew each and everyone.
The Luton that is now, is much faster than before,
It's bigger and much noisier, we don't walk anymore.
I suppose they call it progress, but I much
Prefer the way, it was when I were younger in
The early days.

Margaret R Large

JUST FRIENDS?

My love for you grows more day by day,
I cannot contain it much longer,
How can I tell you I feel this way?
While this yearning gets stronger and stronger.

You are so full of life and passion,
I feel so happy when we are together,
Maybe I will tell you after a fashion,
That I want to be with you forever and ever.

136

You light up my life like no-one before,
I am burning away with desire,
It is of you and only you that I adore,
I want you to take me higher and higher.

This rapture runs deep to the core,
To you, I must make my feelings clearer,
We cannot be just friends anymore,
I sense the day draws nearer and nearer.

Mandy Lee Weir

LONELINESS IS . . .

Loneliness is cold winter days,
It's bathing alone under the hot sun's rays.
Loneliness is the sound of a clock,
It's the quietness of a door, without a knock.
Loneliness is having no-one to care,
It's being unable to really share.
Loneliness is lying awake all night,
It's sitting alone under a soft dim light.
Loneliness is crying alone,
It's no-one to listen at the end of a phone.
Loneliness is a goodbye for a while,
It's saying hello, without a smile.
Loneliness is a long time apart,
It's the death of a loved one, a pain in the heart.

Kathleen McMahon

OLD RED JACKET

Recoiling from another fractured dialogue
Talking to you increases my solitude,
Phone calls fragmenting at the seams.

All communication shuddering to a halt.

In the spaces that follow our painful exchanges
Words reverberate, images scream silently in their confusion.
There is you and me and this monster we have created
Love is no longer able to save us

Photographs and letters lie dormant in an old cardboard box.
Dates of past events flash into my consciousness
Searching for a meaning in this enveloping chaos
Who have we invisibly become?

We arrange to meet, to finalise *things,*
You wear that old red jacket, you look pale,
Your favourite Kafka novel rests on the table,
We order two coffees and shape to talk.

Somewhere along the line something has gone sadly awry.
You tilt your head in that familiar way,
I think about having a cigarette but don't
Small talk starts us off, outside it rains.

The person we need to help us is no longer here
We are alone, the cause of our own anguish.
You tap the table, you have been biting your nails again.
We are locked in this café, lost in the maze of our own creation.

I interject a little humour, you offer half a smile,
You pull some tissues from your pocket,
I light a cigarette, you have one as well.

We order two more coffees.
Unable to part you touch my hand.

Matthew W Jones

SHE'S AN OVERDOSE

I've got a bottle, some pills
And her image in my head
She could cure my ills
I think that's what she said
She's got a lighter
To burn me alive
She was born a fighter
How can I survive?
I could run for miles
Or I could just shout
She walks, she talks, she smiles
And she knocks me out.

Richey Clear

LOVE

What is love?
But an emotion we share.
With a person or persons,
For whom we care.
Love is so different,
In so many ways.
Not one definition,
Not one single phrase.
Can describe the feelings,
That love does impart.
On the soul, the mind.
But especially the heart.

D C N Johnson

LONELINESS INSIDE

Lives of others seem to be filled with delight,
With reasons to live for, and felicity inside,
But, what have I to say is mine, to cuddle,
Laugh with, cry with, to share my sorrows with.

A young, innocent child am I,
What does the term loneliness mean to me?
A lot . . . if you could feel my needs,
Living with pain, fear and grief.
Nothing, if all you require, you have.

I talk not only of money, for money
May buy you a bed but not sleep.
Food but not hunger,
Water but not thirst,
People but not the trust and love you desire.

Still, nobody understands what I am going through,
Or the deepness of my wounds.
The colours of my life are gently fading . . .

So, what am I?
I ask myself,
A reflection in a mirror,
A shadow in the dark,
Or, a book with no story?

Nobody knows what it is like to be denied, all the time.
Just, remembering the dull days, of your life.
All I ask for, is a chance to justify myself,
A little hope, a little ray of light,
To set me on the right path of life.

Seema Jassi

EAT YOUR FOOD!

'Eat your Food!'
Scowl, stare, L-plated daggers.
'I'll turn the cartoons off!'
Two big mouthfuls
'Finished Daddy'
Half covered plate of cold mix displayed
'Eat your food!'
Sad look at the chipless supreme
'I want a drink!'
Negotiable?
'Two more mouthfuls?'
One, two - the drink
Gulp, gulp, gulp
Fred Flintstone's a hypnotist
'Please! Eat your food!'
'I'm not hungry!'
'Two more mouthfuls?'
One, two - 'Can I have afters?'
'Eat your food!'

Mark A Doherty

WAR

Bloody murder fills the air
Screams and gun shots everywhere
Women and children always crying
Men and soldiers forever dying.
Glass and stone hit and hurt
Feet keep running through the dirt.

And in the end the war will cease
But only man shall keep the peace.

E King

DON'T GO MY SON

Like a raindrop on the driest day,
like the sun melting the snow,
I can't stand to watch you drifting away,
it hurts to watch you grow.
This pain is hard to fight,
my heart is crying.
You don't need me anymore at night,
the time between us is dying.
I know that you, feel the pain too,
by the tears that stream from your eyes,
I'm just not ready to let go of you,
I don't want to say goodbye.
Whatever happened to the fun? . . .
. . . Don't go my son.

Lydia Eeles (17)

THE FLU

Shivering, aching and sneezing too,
How can I get rid, of this thing called Flu.

I'd phone the doctor, to seek his advice,
But I've lost my voice, and I'm squeaking like mice.

Feeling tired and worn, I'll just go to bed,
Perhaps it'll clear, this thumping great head.

Two days later, I awake to find,
I'm feeling fit, and have a clear mind.

I jump from my bed, I'm free of the pain,
The sun is shining, I feel well again.

I'd found the remedy, flu gone in two days,
Bed, rest and sleep, really does work - always.

Tricia John

SHIPS IN THE NIGHT

Your friends what were they
But ships in the night
That passed your way.

But on passing you were washed
With their deadly spray.
They called it change of mind
They said
Oh dear, you're not our kind
To this fact we both agree.

Of course we didn't tell you
Straight away.
A little game we had to play
We are sorry if you were hurt
Along the way.
Because this little game,
We just had to play.

The game we played was called
Cat and mouse.
In it we welcomed you
To our house.
You didn't know
How could you tell
We were not those friends
You thought you knew
So well.

A Marshall

A TREE IN WOBURN PARK

Three hundred years, have I stood here,
And many a sight I've seen.
Young men - and old fatigued in fight
Sank down, beneath my green.
Young courtiers with their ladies' fair,
Have stood beneath my boughs
Their arms entwined, soft voices heard,
Exchanging loving vows.
I've never stopped to count the hours,
When children here have played.
In summer sun, they've skipped and ran
Then sheltered in my shade.
And when the changing season brought
A blanket soft and white,
Again their happy voices rang -
Up to the fading light.
When all is quiet, sometimes I think,
I hear a lion roar,
But this is England, fair and green.
And not some foreign shore.
I've lived so many, many, years.
I'm part of history
Where man has gone, here I still stand,
A proud upstanding tree.

Elizabeth M Bartlett

I TRIED

I tried to say the truth
But you didn't understand
I tried to express and explain
But you didn't understand.

So I tried to dream
And make you understand
Or I tried to pray
So God made you understand.

The power that travelled through
Our sleeping souls
Was more than
Our waking minds
Understood.

The power generated
By our searching, expanding minds
Was more than that
Expectorated on our breath,
You knew me in depth
But in the material world
You didn't know me at all.

We were two opposing forces
Because we were the same
And when you gave me something
I already possessed it
Somewhere.

The power that travelled through
Our sleeping souls
Was more than
Our waking minds
Understood.

Joanna Monks

WAR BABIES

Can anyone remember - I guess there are a few
When we were young in Market St - in 1942
(When we were 18 that is!)

The war was on, the men were gone - the pubs all shut at ten
How do you relieve the boredom - when you've really got a yen
(For something else that is!)

Then our prayers were answered - and we all went out to play
For now in little England - were the boys from USA
(Ones with nylons *and* gum that is!)

Who could really blame us - our men were overseas
And no doubt they were playing round - with Mimi, Sophie or Denise
(When they weren't getting shot at that is!)

And now the war is over - our men are back and keen
To be husbands and be fathers - to us kids they've never seen
(War Babies that is!)

Susan Button

THE SEA

Swirling and curling,
The sea,
The unfurling sea.
Drifting along the seashore,
Goes the sea.
Drifting along the seashore.

Skimming and swimming,
The fish.
The wonderful fish.
Swimming and swimming around,
Go the fish,
Swimming and swimming around.

Hannah Pool (8)

OUR SMALL WORLDS
(The tale of an Indonesian 8 year old)

Our small worlds turn paths familiar
Carving out like-minded ways
Ways we feel are ours and different
Simply different shades of grey.

Hardships old no more our lives touch
Fear of hunger can't conceive;
Right to education binds us
Not as fun as life should be.

Polish brush in hand imploring
Big shots, self-absorbed, ignore.
He can't grasp some things before him;
Fortune rides on where you're born.

His small world survival's taught him
Slowly turning raw, hard days.
He'll eke out from endless shortage
Any pleasure to be made.

We face our own share of troubles
Some will hurt while some destroy,
Some we make from yet another
Silver-plattered, boundless choice.

'Have a Coke.' This brings, heart-wrenching
Oh! Such a smile. Bright, wide eyes shining tenderly.
Runs off home to share this rare gift
And his few well-polished pence.

David Langley

147

MUSIC

What music does to me
I can't explain
Soothes my soul, relaxes my brain

The words touch my heart
Doesn't matter who sings
It's the feeling, the joy it brings

Sometimes it can be sad
The story of a life
How they made it
Through trouble and strife

A lot talk of love
And special times
Walks in the park
Memories in their mind.

But it's the tune I tell you
That makes you smile
The melody, makes you forget for a while

It never goes out of fashion
It will be here forever
The old, the young listen
The stupid, the clever.

It's the one thing
We all have in common
Whether we listen, create or play
It can express any feeling
Night or day

So whatever your mood
Put on a song
And feel the music
May it live on!

K Maitland

THE WALK

Arm in arm
They came into the park
And strolled up the Broad Walk

She saw   He saw

The hornbeam subtending   The boys playing
Its green Japanese   Cricket, the children with ice-cream
Pagodas,   Sodas,
The sycamore its winged seeds   Dogs of different breeds,
The ash its bunches of keys.   Families having their teas
The hawthorn attracting bees.   Out, a woman sketching the trees,
A sparrow   An old man with a sparrow
On an old man's hand.   On his hand.

So they passed out, arm in arm,
Of the park they had walked through
Together.

Jean Overton Fuller

CONFUSION

Confusion everywhere!
What to do
Where to go
Who cares?
I care.
I don't know.

Where to turn.
Over here.
Over there.
Somebody,
Please tell me where.

Jane Butland

149

MY OLD SCHOOL

I went to Waller Street Boys,
In the years before the war;
It was next to the Grand, across from the Baths,
Old Luton that now is no more.

The head, his name was Edwards,
He was dreaded by all the boys,
And when he came cycling into the school,
'Soup! Soup!' we'd call out. What a noise!

Knitty Knight, he had the top class,
And taught what we needed to know;
Gobby Hawkins took science, and he was great,
But don't sit yourself in the front row.

We'd get the cane if we did something wrong,
Only right and that was accepted;
We sat up straight and looked at the board,
Our teachers we respected.

When show-people came along into the Grand
We'd peep down from up on the wall,
To boys below tell of fabulous things,
One could see when one's ten feet tall.

Our families were naturally rather poor,
Our clothing was lovingly patched;
Some boys were in leg-irons, one died of TB,
But our spirit could never be matched.

At fourteen we all went out to work,
We left school with just a report
Life was hard, work was long for little reward
Yet with pride for this England, we fought.

Ken J Kilby

FRIENDSHIP

Friends are treasures to have and hold,
But I have a friend whose worth is gold.
Blessed I am with a friend like you,
Kind, considerate, loyal and true.
We've had ups and downs as we've gone along
Sometimes right and sometimes wrong.
We've often laughed at a lot we've done,
Shared joyful occasions and a lot of fun.
Always there, just a call away,
To fetch and carry, come what may.
We've cried together and wiped our tears,
Comforted each other and smoothed the fears.
It takes us both this friendship to make,
Where we both can give and both can take.
An extension you are to my family,
A sincere and precious friend to me.
I'm proud to have you as a friend of mine,
Together to stand the test of time.
Our paths both crossed one blessed day,
As friends we walk through life today.

Carole Wood

A SILENT PRAYER

The battle is over -
The heart stops its beat -
The fountains are weeping
Tomorrow will sleep,
The night's burning candle
Melts slowly in prayer -
Unforgotten memories
Of life's cherished years.

Violet L Sadler

151

SAD I AMS

I am the game I lost last week,
I am the mountain with its mountainless peak,
I am the rebel who was crucified,
I am the lost souls of people who've died,
I am the victim bruised and beaten
I am the last grain of rice to be eaten,
I am the forest burnt to a dust
I am some metal bound to rust,
I am a book with torn out pages
I am poor animals cramped in cages.
I am the man with nothing to be
I am the ball lost out to sea,
I am the world that's frail and weak
I am old bones that painfully creak,
I am life tied up in a knot
I am the dead tree bound to rot,
I feel as if the world's in my face
No sea, no planet, no freedom or space,
Life is like a cotton reel,
Now I'm dead, there's no sadness to feel.

Daniel Jones   (12)

REFLECTIONS

I stood before a mirror in an antique shop one day,
But instead of my reflection, and antiques upon display,
Was a scene of many years ago, a crowded thoroughfare,
The women dressed in crinolines, the men with powdered hair.

The silence was uncanny as they gazed along the street,
Then in the distance I could hear the sound of horses' feet,
They gradually drew nearer, and a cart came into view,
And sitting in it crying was a young girl dressed in blue.

The whispering of the people grew to such a frightening pitch,
Their words were making sense at last 'Burn her, she's a witch.'
At that she lifted up her head, and to my horror I could see
The girl that they were going to burn so long ago was me.

N Biggs

BETRAYAL

Your words fell icily
      into the pool of my content
to lie, glinting in the mud,
      foreign and unabsorbed.

This was no wishing-well benign
      no coins tossed for eager urchins to retrieve.
They shone malignant
      paying the devil with laughter.

You said of course
      you had not meant to harm.
You had not meant . . .
      and yet a trust is gone.

Chagrin, pitch-forked in prods of pain,
      will pass,
and yet I was betrayed.

The moon, tonight, gleams sadly in the pond

M Faithfull

CHILD

Oh child with eyes so full of pain
no need that you should have a name
for as you look through tear-blurred eye
to see your life go flashing by.

Though you be, so unloved, uncared
keeping a secret that goes unshared
body weak from ill neglect
protecting those, who deserve little respect.

Now as you lie in a coffin of white
your memory fading, from the limelight
as all the nation was shocked by the facts
now go about life, by turning their backs.

Forgetting somewhere, there's another in need
spurned by their parent who gave life to the seed
enquiry set up, to find where the fault lies
but before it's concluded another child dies.

Paul James

MEMORIES

He was old, he was matted, and slept on the chair.
His eyes once bright and sparkling, now just seemed to stare,
He dreamt of his youth, when his fur was sleek and shiny.
His eyes could spy a bird or vole, no matter how tiny.

He would leap on the fence, and jump down the wall,
Now if he climbed on a chair, he was likely to fall.
His pleasures in life were just getting less,
Though he still liked his food, but did make a mess.

He could still put his paw inside the tuna tin,
With the skill learnt of old, he'd find scraps in the bin.
But if meat were left out by mistake on the top,
It was safe from his jaws, as he couldn't climb up.

Old age brings its problems to all like the cat,
When your faculties fade, and your figure turns to fat.
But you still have the skills you've acquired your life long,
And your memories remain, and grow ever more strong.

J M Lewis

DANCING STILL

His world has to turn full circle
For spirits like us in flight
To return when memories are recalled
Always pulsating with excessive energy

Some are destined to fill a space
They will appear from the heart
Long ago as part of the pleasure
What happens here is down to you.

Photographs that capture these feelings
Helping us through the toughest time
What we need from each other now
To encourage our survival beyond

So much Heaven on earth to discover
Haunting music unleashes your soul
It all started with goodbye farewell
When we were miles from here dancing still.

Michael Carway

GROWING UP

You scattered clues all over
With your preparations to leave.
And me with my head in the sand
Unprepared to cope with the grief.

No more to hear your laughter
Though it still echoes in my head.
Seeing you turn into a stranger
Whom I still remember with dread.

Will you find what it is you are seeking
On the lonely streets of some town.
Or was that yet another excuse
So you could call your life your own.

I thought you were mine for ever
A loving, exuberant child.
Never dreaming our days were numbered
Outside forces turning you wild.

Stunned with the pain of your going
Now months have passed with no sign
of your face, voice being
Imprinted indelibly on my mind.

Will I see you again this year?
To unknowingly twist the knife
Or will it be Christmas without you
Another first day of the rest of my life.

K A McPhee

THE SELF PITYING BUILDER'S LAST REPLY

In a dimlit saloon,
where sad guys look for room,
An' a piano sings well out of tune,
Spoke a red-eyed ole man,
'Sure I've done what I can,
I lived life to the full, in the boom.'

Now site workers are lost,
though their souls pay the cost,
As fat cats sup up cream - from a bowl,
to the ching of a till,
here we empty our swill,
All we hear some ole dog rake a howl.

Slap some gold on the bar,
Lord, it doesn't go far
hear the coughs of the choir all around,
though there's only a few,
but God look at the spew,
an' the carrots that speckle the ground.

In this hovel they fart,
'tis Nature's crude part,
An' none here live a life of illusion,
but life's rivers must flow,
if you need you must go,
to the fall out of such an effusion.

But don't cast us a line,
for we really are fine,
An' warm words be a great loss of breath,
See we have a friend,
to all we can send,
An' he drinks with the Angel of Death.

I Maclaren

157

MOTHER'S LOVE

To Me You are loving and caring, and the world's very best Mother,
To Me You are perfect and unique, you are like no other.
To Me You give me your time, you listen, then advise,
To Me You give me your love so freely, you are a comfort and so wise.

To You You are my best friend, and that I'm sure you know,
To You Of all the years to come, I hope our friendship will grow,
To You I have to say, I love you, Mum, much more than I can say,
To You For I know it will always be that way, forever and a day.

K Fountain

THE EIGHTIES REVISITED

Mumbling strange accented oaths
He rams his fists down others' throats
And ends with violence to achieve
All that discourse can't conceive
So countless lads in sullen streets
Fantasise of macho feats
And the clay brains with XR3i
Dream of guns and how to die,
And Arnie's victims grunt and groan
Adding weight to the testosterone;
As video rentals soar on high
Arnie's pecs bestride the sky.

Graham Rankin

MY FATHER IS HITLER

Father sits
Alone again.
Thinking of all the men he could have been.
No tears
Or violins.
I hate him with all I am worth.

Bad dreams
of dead dogs.
(We tried to tame his angered ambitions).
No more
Kitchen jokes.
He hid his laughter in the freezer.

And now (and again)
My father is Hitler.
And now (and again)
My father is Hitler.

A sly wife
With long sighs.
Yet I was a breaker of the bridge.
A life-size
Suicide.
And I still no longer exist.

I was the breaker of the bridge.
And I still no longer exist.

Zoe-Christina Smith

WITH OR WITHOUT YOU

Here and over there,
people will silently stare
it doesn't matter 2 them,
with or without u,

> Up on the hillsides
> whilst down on chocolate taste buds
> it doesn't matter 2 them,
> with or without u

Show them your eyes
and let them see the reflection of me
it won't matter 2 them,
with or without u,

> Trodden thoughts
> as x marks our spot
> will it matter 2 u,
> if I'm with or without u,

If I wash my soul
and all danger walk away from,
wait 4 judgement day
and our kingdom to come,
would it matter 2 u
if u are with or without me or
if u are with or without them.

Khalid Latif

ONLY MAKE BELIEVE

Brilliant, Bold, sunset rays
Emerging through a winter haze
Sinking slowly, sinking *Red* -
Symbolic life now lies dead.

Shadows fall on sleepless eyes
Where fear is locked and cannot hide
The inward dread of mindless sounds
As death's dark friends start spinning round;

Voices call out from the mists
Where sweat succumbs to hatred's kiss
To make the legs melt under strain
While darkness feeds the tortured brain.

Black! - The only colour - *Black!*
Where rainbows end and feelings lack
The solar thoughts so far away
Because sweet death will not decay;

In a million years, it seems
An orange sky will come between
The borders of the inner mind
To grate the peel of death's own rind.

Heroic Sun! Where gold resides
Caress the skyline and blot out our pride
And paint in all the coloured scenes
In this, our world of *Make Believe.*

Stephen John

AUTUMN LEAVES

Autumn leaves begin to fall
Some brown, some red, some gold,
They form a carpet on the ground.
The trees look bare and cold.

The Summer blooms are fading fast
The earth seems calm and still
The surge of life is there no more
And Autumn has her will.

She abdicates for Winter's reign
That long, long, sleep, until
Sweet Spring comes bounding back again,
Please God she always will.

E Gaskin

THE MOON

As I stood alone gazing,
. Out my window at the sky,
Behind the steeple light blazing,
It belonged to the moon up high.

A beam of light crept in view,
Getting clearer by the second,
In all its beauty, I saw I knew,
Its face to me it beckoned.

Passing clouds passed away,
So its form could show light,
And the hours pass to day,
Its fight over with the night.

Me, a tiny human staring back,
Gazing from my window alone,
Remembering the love I lack,
Bless this moon, on its throne.

C Gordon

THE LONELY HEART

I travel alone and do my part
To ease and heal this lonely heart
Someone to talk to, someone to care
Perhaps to love, at least to share
The lonely aching path I tread
The unending days I seem to dread
One day who knows, somewhere I'll find
Another soul who needs peace of mind
And maybe then at last I'll know
The joy of sharing that brings a glow
Could you be the one to enter my life
A friend, a lover, to share the strife
Someone, somewhere, right from the start
To ease the burden of this lonely heart
We'll find such joy, such peace from pain
Happiness, contentment, and laughter again
And when at last the sun shines thro'
In this lonely heart, as I know it can do
I will be so proud to stand and say
This lonely heart has flown away.

Joan Walker

A GROUSE FROM A HANDICAPPED CHILD

Are you a handicapped child like me?
Are you scorned and laughed at like me?
Is your mind a bit damaged like mine?
Are your limbs and thoughts like mine
all muddled and not very fine?
All your thoughts and limbs are in line,
My limbs and thoughts take time
to move on a very fine line,
I would if I could think quick
Then people would not think me so thick,
Nor would they jump and take the mick,
If I could just think so quick,
But I can never be normal like you
and stand in the rush hour queue,
Or read the papers and find the plots
to see if so and so copped his lot,
I can never be married and have kids
or have a farm and look after pigs,
I can never have problems and strifes
or be a nurse and help save a life,
But there is only one grouse I've got
and that's with all you lot,
Must you treat me like a tiny tot?
And pretend I'm still in a cot.

Mick Terri

JUST A THOUGHT . . .

If I stood on the outside
for all of my life
who would listen if I spoke

If I move to the inside
and stand with the masses
who would I speak to

164

If I stand with those people
and then get lost
who will help me find my path

So I'll stand here on the outside
And I'll listen when I speak
then none need hear my screams.

Paula Stedman

MEMORIES

A sky full of sunshine,
A church full of song
The day of the wedding,
With feelings so strong.

The bride of the moment
With radiant smile,
Walks with her father,
Down that long aisle.

The vows are then taken,
The register signed,
Then cars to reception,
Where all wined and dined.

With music and laughter,
And talk of the past,
The magic starts fading,
The time goes so fast.

Good luck and God bless you,
Have great years to share,
A day to remember
From one who was there.

Geoff Elmer

LITTLE ANGELS

Newspapers strewn across the floor
A cushion lodged behind the door.
Videos scattered all around
Their cardboard covers can't be found.

Flower petals in a pile
On the carpet - don't make me smile.
A ball of wool wound round the chair,
The settee looks the worse for wear.
And strawberry jam - so sticky and spread
On everything - except the bread.
Biscuit crumbs upon the mat
Whatever's happened to our cat.

'Have we had a burglary?'
No, just Marc, Gem, and Laura
Our toddlers three
Have been for tea.

Shirley Adams

ALL'S FAIR IN LOVE AND WAR?

Love is divided between one and one
Mostly decided by things that you've done
Though there is pain
Like summer rain
As soon as its started it's gone
War is decided by who has the guns
Children are dying, the innocent ones
All's fair in Love and War?
Look a bit closer, see if you're sure
War might seem fair to those who survive
But what think the people no longer alive . . ?

Louise Farrell

THE BUPA HOSPITAL

Even in a private hospital
New built, soft lit,
Carpeted with courtesy;
The bones of the terror of sickness and death
Are sticking out of the soft covers
And rattling me.

Why does my friend lie so still, so low
So awkwardly placed
In the torture bed?
Equipped with dials and knobs and tubes
Machines grinding the soft tissue of life:
Clumsy I knock the yellow bag
Sickeningly oozing from the catheter.

We take tea and chat
As if nothing were wrong.
When nurses perform
Some private outrage
I go out to a side room
Where leaflets lie:

What To Do When Someone Dies

Not my problem, today, thank God.
My friend is lucky -
She's getting better;
But I still leave cramped and cold
With the gaping fear of disintegration and death.

Caroline Saunders

THE LAKE OF FIRE!

The other night I dreamt a dream
Which caused my heart to ache!
A heavenly light sent down its beam
And took me to a lake!
Upon the Lake of Fire's shores
A crowd of people stood -
As if both time and space took pause
Inside Hell's neighbourhood!
I walked among the figures crammed
So tightly side by side
And knew these souls as lost and damned
Yet not one soul now cried!
It seemed the time for tears had passed -
Salvation wasn't theirs -
Thus from the first unto the last
God spurned their sighs and prayers!
And so they stood, and stared and stared,
And waited Judgment Day -
As if no longer deathly scared,
But yielding, come what may . . .
An angel flew above my head
Then landed next to me,
Then wiped my tears, and softly said,
'Come Now to Calvary!'
I saw the Saviour on the Hill
And climbed the path above
To see His body, bleeding still -
God's Lamb, the King of Love . . .
The angel said, *'Behold the Man . . .*
If Christ can't save you . . . Nobody can. . .'

Denis Martindale

NOT UNLESS

Tread not the sacred place where once we kissed,
unless your heart still yearns, for yearnings missed.
Read not the poets' works we pondered long,
unless a tear can find the word belong.
Lilt not the lover's songs we sang together,
unless your soul belongs to mine forever.
Dream not the dreams we dreamt in summer's clover,
unless your garb is palled as my own cover.

Weep not for long on hilltop whence we part,
unless you would deny me rest, sweetheart.

J E Burton

PEOPLE RHYTHM

We are stormed by people's traumas
Dragged along by their problems
And anchored by our self-respect and trust
And when a wave turns to drowning
We swim along
In others' deepest threat
And save each other with
Presence and glances

My dependence on you
Fires me to stand on my own
And be in the dance circle of people rhythm
Bouncing off and being part of
Our celebration.

Sandra Cooper

169

NATURE'S CONFINEMENT

Spring is pushing gently
For nature to give birth
Winter abandoning her barriers
Makes way for Mother Earth

'Tis nature's reckoning to set her months
For her delivery on time
When spring is born it truly is
Wonderfully sublime

When spring burst forth its every seam
Exploding in the sun
Nature's labour fought through winter
Has only just begun

Perspiring in the morning dew
Nature holds a strong foundation
Spreading evenly her fruits to bear
For her yearly restoration.

The weather glides in warmly
From all corners of the earth
Awakening strong signs of life
To assist a speedy birth.

With the elements in attendance
And all the birds that sing
Nature has delivered
A season we call spring.

Honora Lowther

THE ROAD TO SWINESHEAD

Elder-flower, hawthorn, crab-apple and sloe,
Dog roses and willow, this ancient hedgerow,
It's been there for centuries with nowhere to go,
On the road that leads you to Swineshead.

Through hot summer's air, a distant dog cries,
The meadow larks call, a song thrush replies,
A crescendo of crows take to wing with a sigh,
On the road that leads you to Swineshead.

Ah, village of beauty, the Church, the Five Bells,
Never knowing romance you bestow,
On the townsfolk like me who succumb to your spells,
On this road with nowhere to go.

Steve Syratt

TO LISE

A woman stands where, yesterday, my baby daughter stood;
Beholding you, I know that now you've entered adulthood.
For eighteen very precious years you've blessed me with your smile
And knowing you and loving you has made my life worthwhile.

Your childhood years, to mould or mar, will never more be mine;
Some other love will walk with you - your future Valentine.
Your hopes, your dreams of happiness will gently bless your smile
And seeing you and loving you will make my life worthwhile.

Of unseen days I cannot know but pray that you will find
Your destiny, God's plan for you, fulfilment, peace of mind;
A man to love and motherhood, to richly bless your smile
And knowing, seeing, loving you, will make my life worthwhile

G E Shepherd

HENLEY ROYAL REGATTA

If you had come to the Royal Regatta,
This is what you might have seen:
Hats and dresses,
Flowing tresses,
Caps and blazers,
Chaps and geysers,
Picnic hampers,
Pimms and champers,
Lots and lots of idle chatter,
And then some racing in between.

I wish you had come to the Royal Regatta
Then, of course, you could have seen:
Sparkling river,
Flags a-quiver,
Rippling muscles,
Rowing tussles,
Pools and splashes,
Crabs and clashes,
And it would not really matter
About the talking in between.

I am glad you came to the Royal Regatta
For now you can say that you have been
One of the faces
Watching the races;
One of the chaps
Under the caps;
One of the girls
With hat and curls;
And that, amid the fun and chatter,
You, too, were a part of the Henley scene.

K G Burton

172

KIM

She came from nowhere . . .
Lost, abandoned, one wet Bank Holiday
And so it was . . .
The village came to know her as the stray.
No scavenger . . .
Her frantic search for food was bound to fail
And as time passed . . .
Her slender body told its own sad tale.
Yet there were some like me . . .
So saddened by her misery and her plight
Would offer food . . .
And she would look with longing then take fright
Until that special day . . .
My birthday by the merest quirk of fate
As if by hands unseen . . .
The dog was guided through my garden gate.
I knelt to greet her . . .
Hands outstretched to show I meant no harm . . .
And softly spoke . . .
To tell her there was no need to feel alarm,
And cautiously . . .
She made her first brave step to lick my face
And then it was . . .
The dog and I both knew . . . She'd found her place.

Betty Searby

SEEDS

Little seeds,
Flowers or weeds?
No-one will know
Until they grow.

Shaun Farrington (5)

UNTITLED

Interpret to me
The colours of this season
Who painted them?
And for what reason?
Did he imagine
The autumn he would create
And add a secret
To the palette?

For although
The colours are a death
There is life beneath
Waiting to draw breath
And although
There is a space of time
On the verge of crying
There is no denying

Kimberley Kennedy

YEARS

As the tears fell from her eyes,
The anger rose from within
Hurt appeared in her heart,
As the tears fall to the floor.

Each cheek was wet,
Her eyes were raw.
Loving someone who was by the door,
Closing herself to feel pain no more.

The tears were washed away,
As the thought of life entered,
She had more to give him,
Than just tears of sorrow.

Joy came from her heart,
Sunshine smiled from her face.
Together they can make,
Heaven and earth a wonderful place.

S Ma'Po-Tear

SEASONS

Summertime I like the best
Don't like staying in to rest
For when it's fine, I go outside
Get on a bus, go for a ride
Take the dog out for a walk
Meet with people, stop and talk
When it's dull I stay indoors
And rush to do those household chores

Wintertime I hate it so
For then there is no place to go
No more sitting in the park
Days are cold, will soon be dark
Then when going out for walks
Nobody stops, nobody talks
Then most days I stay indoors
No need to rush the household chores

J M James

THE REACHING OF RIGHTNESS

Lines not yet formed
already exist
in the chaliced chamber
of my being,
where they wait for me
to force them into flower
from the greenhouse of heated labours
that only I can germinate.
Shoots surge up
in the peat of struggling thoughts
and lay on the page
like testing seedlings
gauging the suitability of their bed.
Words slip into allocated order
and move around the darkness of my mind
on the brightness of the addicted paper,
until I feel the final precision
of every lounging letter.
Then a pervading smile of petals
blooms in a celebration of creation
as vines from every aspect of me
entwine
in a timeless moment
where we discover together
the sweet wine
of this reaching of rightness.

K Kirkman

RAW WAR

Now that I'm well past three score and ten
methinks it's time I took up the pen.
There's one certain word that I abhor
It has only three letters and it spells war.

Just think how much smaller that book would be
The one we call a dictionary.
For one thing there would be no ranks
no planes, destroyers and army tanks.

No bombs, guns and searchlights
All in our beds sleeping safely at nights,
No uniforms, kit bags nor boots to shine
everything peaceful and just fine.

No aircraft carriers and submarines
No Army, Navy or Royal Marines
No stand to attention and salute
Just all of us dressed in a civvy suit.

No awards or medals for campaigns,
No war cemeteries filled with Names
No need to sing 'Keep the home fires burning'
No loved ones not returning.

No silence at the Cenotaph
All of us on a peaceful path.
So the dictionary would have a different look
It would be a much thinner book.

Notice that this word called *war*
When reversed spells out *raw*.
Only when human life is past
will there be peace on earth at last.

C H Green

REMEMBERING

Hours later alone
I trace our steps up and into
and linger, gazing
longingly at the crumpled array
At pillows, sheet and quilt I stare
deceived by memory that never
fades or loses its tenacity

My eyes recall your beloved face
beneath, above
Head pillowed on your chest
listening to the life in you
living, loving body safe
protected in the firmness of
your arm's embrace

Recalling, reliving the sublimity
of skin dissolved in unity
Bonded, welded in love, by love
legs arms hands and fingers entwined

Empty of you and the way you fill
this space, this place
is the heart and centre of my loneliness

Lynn Gostelow

LOVE

I sought love in the distant hills,
But they were bare.
I sought love in the silent woods,
No-one was there.
I sought love by the rolling sea,
But no-one came to comfort me.

So home I went, and there I found
The love I sought was all around.
The touch of his hand as he drew me in.
His voice as he said 'You've been away
But how I hope you're here to stay.'

I had no need to climb a hill,
Or find a wood, or go to sea.
For love was waiting here for me.

F E Bridle

COLOURS

Oh, crystal waters
you sparkle divine.
Your diamonds are dancing
the songs in my mind.

Oh, dazzling sunlight
you shine down so fine,
on the mirrors of the waters
on the reflections of my mind.

Lilac like a lily
as green as the grass,
blue skies and misty dales.
As yellow as the sun
or as pink as laughter
rainbows and silent oceans.

What colours you may find
such delight
in sight and mind.

K Lansfield

PRESENCE

We kiss as lovers
And talk as friends
But this is where it starts to end.
You tell me I'm pretty
And I wonder why
This seems to be the obligatory lie.
I tell you my warning
You say you can cope
I starve myself and feed off hope.
Fine around others
With games I play
Alone is where I lose my way.
One kiss feels good
Your hand there too.
Blinded by memories - if only you knew.
I look through you
It's him I see.
I'm such a bitch. I'm glad it was me.
I hear you murmur
Pure pleasure you show
But I see him ignoring my 'No.'
I curl up tight
Just affection I need
Can't open my mouth or my soul will bleed.
You've done nothing wrong
So I just shut my eyes.
Can't speak of this pain, so I silently cry.

Anna Strickland

TOGETHERNESS FOR THE SECOND TIME

The fire crackles
And the flames dance around the room.
The room is filled with magic.
A cosy light reflects on each of the cottage walls.

The old man's pipe
Fills the room with its musty smell,
Its own rugged smell,
That makes you feel distant and tired.

The room is silent
As the old man thinks of his wife,
He clutches her photograph
Feeling alone.

His wife, now dead,
May also have memories of the man,
The man she loved,
her soul still lives in the room.

The man now sleeps
An everlasting sleep.
The man's and woman's souls are now together,
Together in the room.

The flames die,
Just as the man and woman died.
The pipe smell fades, just as they fade,
The souls linger in the smoke.

Natalie Usher

THE GAME

She filled his eyes with errant dreams
His fingers curled her hair
From every line, her innocence
Eyes, long lashed, straight and blue
No aching heart could bear.

'Oh marry me, when you grow up.'
It was their joke, their thing
'I will, I will' her answer squealed
'Sooner then,' the cynic cooed
'We'll book it for the spring.'

The Amaryllis came and went
When winter came with fervent sighs
His plighted troth remained
Playing hard the fragile game
He drank youth through her eyes.

Relentlessly dumb vanity
O'erplayed the waiting hand
Within that angel's mind, a doubt
That it could not be carried out
A myth of trickled sand.

So she then touched his spotted palm
'It's time for me to go.'
'Grandad, I cannot marry you.'
Times cruel time had won the game
He looked away, then muttered soft
'I know. I know. I know.'

C W Macdonald

THE SEA OF DESPAIR

I swim in the sea of despair,
a place between nothing and nowhere.
The water is salty tears
that people have cried over countless years.
I try to swim but I'm floundering
I try to stay afloat but I'm drowning.
Drowning in tears I've cried
because of the love I'm denied,
because the centre of my attention
wants nothing of my affection.
The barrier is too strong to break down
and so I drown.

The water stings my eyes - makes me blind
It stops me breathing and warps my mind.
I want you to hold out your hand
and carry me to dry land
but all there is, is the endless sea,
a watery tomb surrounding me.
I don't want to join the others who've died
in this sea of suicide
But my despair is because of you
and my will to live is because of you too
Yet which way up, which way down
I can't tell, so I drown.

Ian Morgan

WESTWARDS

Towards the dusk, under an arch
Of oaks, cradling the growing dark
In their branches. Spots of spiteful rain
Spatter against the glass again
To remind me that this is Wales.
Gloucester, beloved of Gurney,
Lies behind me, as does his grass-grown grave;
Ahead, the litany of most-favourite place names.
Bwlch, above a sweeping climb
Of Alpine turns, time after time
Draws comment for its lack of vowel
From English lips, as does, in lesser wise,
Llanspyddid; Cwmwysg, where crows fly
Over high earth and concrete dam
Has hump backed bridge of earlier age:
This Old Road crosses centuries, cultures,
As well as miles. I head for a dearer destination
Than mere time and place suggest,
Somewhere held in heart's deepest pulse.
Through the dark I feel presence of chapel
Standing foursquare across the valley
Amidst apostolic ash and yew;
Strange the mix of God and myth
In Celtic lands where evil abounds in hedges
And dark woods, unacknowledged
Yet perceived, nowhere stronger than here,
Just over the border in the half light
On the cusp of dark day, and night.

Patrick Taylor

PS I LOVE YOU

Hello my dear, how's the weather?
It's raining here can't get much wetter.
I suppose you are missing me
'cause I am missing you.
Still I'll be home soon, don't fret.
So it's bye for now etc etc
                    PS. I love you.

Dearest darling it's me again
Just a line to tell you how I am.
Excuse the writing I'm in the bath
if you could see me now I bet you would laugh.
Well I'll finish here; time to go.
Oh yes, I'll phone you tomorrow.
                    PS. I love you.

I always enjoyed those letters you sent,
the words so varied, the love so meant.
The themes changed
the places too.
But consistent through and through
after all else.
                    PS. I love you.

Once again things have changed,
The people, the places,
new friend, new faces.
Can the ending stay the same?
It's still the same for me
could it be the same for you?
                    PS. I love you
                    PPS. Do you still love me?

George Hackett

THE GOLD BAND

As I was out walking down a country lane
I heard a gentle tapping upon a window pane,
I looked over yonder a cottage I could see
an old withered hand was beckoning to me.
I walked up a crooked path to a door opened wide
an old woman stood there and bid me come inside.
The room smelt musty a fire was glowing bright,
A candle on the mantelpiece gave off an eerie light.
She sat down beside me and reached out her hand,
From off of her pale finger she took a gold band.
I want you to have this and wear as your own
gone now is my loved one and I am all alone.
She made me feel quite humble because she was so kind,
I had to refuse I hope she did not mind.
Sadness veiled her ashen face as she tightly took my hand,
Pleading with me gently to take her gold band.
I sat and took tea with her from off a cloth of lace,
Then she bid me a fond farewell a smile upon her face.
I walked back down the crooked path and as I glanced back,
The cottage was no longer there only a run-down old shack.
Glancing down quickly to look at my hand
there it was still shining a lovely gold band.
Then the truth dawned on me that my charming host
had turned out to be just a lonely ghost.
I still go walking down that quiet country lane
hoping that the cottage will appear again.
I sometimes can feel her gently take my hand
lovingly touching her lovely gold band.

B J Day

AN EMPTY HOUSE

No eyes pleading for 'just a crust,'
no paw held out in a gesture of trust.
No warm body pressed against your knees,
no mad scamper for the nearest trees.
No cold wet nose to brush your hand,
no look that says 'I understand.'
No comforting presence when you're feeling low,
as the front door opens no barking 'Hello.'
No smell of wet fur and a bedraggled look,
no claws on line, no lead on the hook.
No long hairs left on stairs and carpet,
no rucked up covers in his basket.
No great big sigh as he falls asleep,
    No Kibber.

Ann P Chivers

IT'S SO HARD

It's not easy to see what others think of you,
but you know what you think of them.
It's so easy to think that you've got it right,
not like the other men.

So many believe the grass can be greener,
and struggle to the other side.
So few are content with what they have,
and think fortune will arrive on the tide.

Hard times are not known until you've had them,
and few of us will ever see.
Hard times are known by a few poor souls.
Thank you Lord for not including me.

Jonquill

MEMORIES

I remember, I remember
So many things. I am over 80 years old
But most of all I remember
My first visit to Lakeland
When I was but 20 years old.
Newly engaged to my love
We saw the daffodils, newly spring
From the earth.
Not to be forgotten, despite his death
Many years ago.

F Wilkinson

FAMILY TREE - 13 YEARS AND STILL COUNTING

In this room where my mother died,
I wonder how many like me have cried,
How many tears have blessed this floor,
And empty souls unlocked the door,
Which leads to a world, bathed in cold daylight,
That cuts right through you, so stark, so bright,
And how many more just as me,
Watched a leaf gently fall from their family tree.

Oh, the tears that welled and stung my eyes,
Were hidden behind a brave disguise,
'Til a soft voice whispered, 'Don't be ashamed of your grief,'
As from my shoulder I brushed the fallen leaf.
With my emotional aegis now ripped apart,
Revealing a fragile, crystal heart,
I uncovered my face for the world to see,
How intense was the love death stole from me.

Simon Darnell

LESSONS OF LIFE

Life is a miracle,
Every new day,
Warmth of the sunshine,
Freshness of May.

Life is developing,
New skills to learn,
Acquiring knowledge,
Respect to earn.

Life is a challenge,
Taking a chance,
Facing each problem,
No backward glance.

Life is rewarding,
Memories to keep,
Loved ones to cherish,
Feelings run deep.

Life is forgiveness,
Differences past,
No bitter feelings,
Friendships that last.

Life is accepting,
Rich man and poor,
Everyone equal,
Hatred no more.

Life is believing,
Trust in mankind,
Hope for the future,
Brings peace of mind.

Maureen Dracup

THE DECEASED ON THE LOSS OF AN ONLY PET

We did not know his coming,
    Our bob-tailed, ginger stray.
We only never questioned
    That he had come to stay.
For he assumed his welcome
    With unselfconscious gaze -
A look of utter love and trust,
    And matched by loving ways.
He'd always give us welcome,
    Whatever hour we came,
And show us true affection -
    This cat without a name.
This cat - or changeling - what was he?
    He surely was unique.
There could not be another -
    We don't intend to seek.
Indeed, we did not seek this one,
    Or any of like breed.
He came unsought, in answer to
    An unsuspected need.

We do not know his going.
    They found him in the drive,
His eyes upturned, which had bewitched,
    When he had been alive.
I'd planned to shelter him tonight
    From noise the fireworks made,
But now he lies much nearer them -
    Oh, Choosey - don't be afraid!

Olive Summerfield

I'LL COME QUIETLY

These words have come leaking out,
About a man who's a china cup.
His little world goes *round and round.*
And the only thing that once came down,
Was a flying saucer,
Who married the cup and produced a daughter.
Born with a silver spoon on the side.

Her father took a steady job,
In order to earn a couple of bob.
But the daughter's hopes were bigger than his,
So she joined a posh tea service.
Much to her half-baked mother's pride.

Once inside the upper class,
The daughter got to know a glass.
'Won't you stay with me for all time?'
Said the glass with a whine.
Could be all white, defiantly dry.

'Oh no,' she said 'for I'm not fit,
To be seen at a suave banquet.
I'm from a lowly cup and saucer,
And you can't get any coarser.'
So she left with a tear in her eye.

She spurned the glass, although he loved her.
For holey wedlock with a colander.
But although the former was far more posher,
They still met up, in the dish washer.

Ian Dixon

PENNY

Tired and tearful is the girl,
For once her heart filled with love,
Soared higher and higher like the peaceful dove.
Her heart filled with content,
As if from heaven this great feeling was sent.
She gave to him something she'd never before relent
The home she built and kept clean,
For him she'd become anything.
For him she breathed and would die,
For that's how she felt inside.
But now shattered by the truth of a thousand lies,
She still breathes but inside has died.

Angela Fagan

OUT OF AFRICA

I'm an unshy sort of violet from Africa's land.
In compost, in pot, here I proudly stand. '
My family's coloured pink, red and deep blue
With nice yellow centres - a quite motley crew.

There are those who won't like me 'cos of Apartheid
For, sometimes you see my colour is white.
We flowers do not mind about colour you see
We only display them to welcome the bee.

But humans are cruel and very unfair
When it comes to the colour about which they care.
Though it says in their Bible 'God made man one day'
Nowhere can I find what shade was the clay.

I know about soil - it can be yellow or brown
And occasionally red, for my roots to go down.
Man should see more sense (for he's always had sight)
There are very few places where the clay is pure white!

A P Woodall

MY LIFELINE

How good it is to hold you
Each and every day
How good it is to listen
To what you have to say

I could not be without you
So all my love I send
I won't ever live without you
for you are my best friend

You listen to all my worries
And when I'm feeling sad
You listen to all my joys
You must think me quite mad

But I will never live without you
I will never be on my own
For you are my endless lifeline
My best friend - the phone.

Angela Barrett Cordiner

TO PAUL WITH LOVE

Paul you tried to take your life last night,
And in your mind, you believed this was right.
Where do I fit in that lonely life of yours,
Perhaps I don't I'm really not too sure.

I feel so safe with you, tell me why?
When all you seem to do, is make me cry.
I need you so much Paul, I really do,
If only you could need me too.

I need you to hold me, close to you,
And to say those three words, I love you.
I need you to make me laugh, when I am sad,
And to take my hand, when things are bad.

I need you to tickle me, when we fool around,
So I can tickle you too, and hear those sounds.
I need your company late at night
To talk aloud, when the time is right.

Can't you see, you're breaking my heart,
I know people have tried to tear us apart.
But we have succeeded where people went wrong,
Our love is so binding, it will be strong.

I needed you yesterday, I need you today,
So please Paul, face up to life, don't run away,
For I will be there, right by your side,
Until you are ready to make me your wife.

Michelle Simpkins

DESCRIPTION OF LOVE

Describe your favourite colour
And the reason for that choice
Think how your favourite singer sounds
And why you like that voice
What makes a certain type of food
Taste better than the rest?
And tell me why one special wine
Is certainly the best.

Which precious metal do you like?
And which gem means the most?
Do you like bread and butter?
Or margarine on toast?
A sniff of scent or aftershave
Can mean so very much
But can a question from the past
Deny a loving touch?

Deliberate and question things
Ensure your thoughts are true
Make sure that you feel happy
In all you say and do
When you have found the answers
And they fit you like a glove
You haven't just found happiness
You've just described your true love.

Terry Snelling

LIFE'S MEMORIES

Laying awake at night,
watching patterns of light,
shifting across my ceiling,
I drift back to days gone by,
touching memories of my life.

I'm a child,
and the world's so big
There's so much to do,
so many trees to climb,
I'll never have the time.

Teenage years,
a spurt of growth.
I'm now a man,
or at least I think so,
so much to do, so little time left.

Middle twenties
steady job,
money to spare,
I know what I want,
I'm almost there.

Now I'm here,
my goals are fixed.
I have all I want,
and more than I deserve,
for I have you.

Now you are with me,
a new life begins,
and time, what does it matter,
as long as we are together,
and so we shall always be.

Gary Green

MADAME SHOP ASSISTANT

Madame Shop Assistant you're the cutest I've ever seen
And from the way you stock the canned food I can tell
you're the best there's been.

I can remember when I first saw you pricing up the meat
My heart turned to water and slowed and skipped a beat.

I try to get your attention knocking over products by the score
But it's always some other shop assistant who tidies up the floor.

Sometimes I dream that everyone is gone and we are by ourselves
But even then you don't notice me and keep on packing shelves.

I've studied how you work the till and all your different moods
It seems we will always be separated by a stack of frozen foods.

David Williams

THE NILE

The great river calm and beautiful,
Little fish swimming up and down,
Suddenly a great pounding wave floods the ground,
After a long wait the river calms,
People sailing and animals swimming,
Night falls with a sunset.

Steven Miller (10)

TO THOSE WHO DIED

We give our thanks to those who died
Also our thanks to them who cried
When dealing with a loved one lost.
We now remember, count the cost.
To them!

Our Heroes lost!

Ginney

INFORMATION

We hope you have enjoyed reading this book - and that you will continue to enjoy it in the coming years.

If you like reading and writing poetry drop us a line, or give us a call, and we'll send you a free information pack.

Write to

Anchor Books Information
1-2 Wainman Road
Woodston
Peterborough
PE2 7BU